Monograph Book

ANTIBACTERIAL ACTIVITY OF NATURAL AND COMMERCIAL HONEY

Editors

Dr. Mustafa Salah Hasan
University of Fallujah, College of Veterinary Medicine, Anbar, Iraq.

Dr. Reyam Abdul Khuder Mohammed Jassam
A–Mustaqbal University College, Department of Radiology Techniques, Hilla, Iraq.

Dr. P. Saranraj
Department of Microbiology, Sacred Heart College (Autonomous), Tirupattur, Tamil Nadu, India

Published by

JPS Scientific Publications
India

Published by

JPS Scientific Publications, Tamil Nadu, India.
E.mail: jpsscientificpublications@gmail.com
Website: www.jpsscientificpublications.com

Published in India.

International Standard Book Number (ISBN): 978-93-91342-21-0

JPS Scientific Publications also publishes its books in a variety of Electronic formats. Some content that appears in print may not be available in Electronic formats. For more information visit our publication website www.jpsscientificpublications.com

ISBN: 978-93-91342-21-0

Contents

1. INTRODUCTION

Honey has been highly appreciated as an alimentary product, and has been largely used, since ancient times, as well as in cosmetic manufacturing. Honey is a sugary substance obtained from the nectar of the flowers or from the secretions which come from or lie on the living parts of the plant and which honey bees crop, transform and combine with their own specific substances, and store in the honeycomb of the beehive. Honey is a product extremely rich in sugars of which glucose and fructose are outstanding. It also possesses vitamins, mineral salts and microorganisms in honey have long been used to control the spoilage of honey. Microorganisms in honey may influence quality and safety. Due to the natural properties of honey and control measures in the honey industry, honey is a product with minimal types and levels of microbes. The microbes of concern in honey are primarily yeasts and spore-forming bacteria (Weston, 2000).

Honey forms part of the traditional medicine in many cultures. According to Gomez - Caravaca (2006), antibiotic resistance emerged as major global (Amabile Cuevas, 2006) problem hospitals, especially in the clinical treatment of ulcers, bed sores, burns, injuries and surgical wounds. The antibacterial properties of honey may be particularly useful against bacteria which have developed resistance to many antibiotics. For example, *Staphylococcus aureus*, which is a major cause of wound sepsis in hospitals. Honey is thus an ideal topical wound dressing agent in surgical, infections, burns and wound infections (Armstrong and Otis, 1995).

Honey has been extensively used as healing agent throughout the human history in addition to its widespread usage as popular food. Honey is a sweet substance produced as a food source mainly from the nectar and secretions of plants by honey bees. Honey is used to feed bees during the winter (Jaganathan and Mandal, 2009). For centuries, honey has been used as food and as natural medicine, being prescribed by physicians of many ancient cultures for the treatment of a wide variety of ailments. The art of apiculture and the benefits of honey have been known. Since, the Egyptian first dynasty (Nicholson and Shaw, 2000) and ancient Greeks used honey as a sweetener (Brothwell and Brothwell, 1969). In classical Greece, laws concerning apiculture were suggested and Plato included honey in their concept of a healthy diet (Skiadas and Lascaratos, 2001). The use of honey in folk medicine is thought to be as old as civilization, but in recent times there has been a renaissance in interest in its use as a medicinal product. The colour of honey can vary from clear to dark amber according to its floral source and mineral content and it has a close relationship with its flavour and quality (Jaganathan and Mandal, 2009). Honeys may be viscous liquids or even solid with differing honeys identifiable by their colour, flavour, crystallization and the presence of pollen grains in honey sediment (Alves Da Silva *et al.*, 2006).

Honey is mainly composed of water and sugar (about 96%) with the remainder being substances such as amino acids, enzymes, minerals, flavonoids, phenolic acids, ascorbic acid, carotenoid-like substances, organic acids, and several other compounds (White and Subers, 1963; Tan *et al.*, 1989; Alves Da Silva *et al.*, 2006). D-fructose and D- glucose are the predominant sugars. Sucrose occasionally exceeds 1 % of the total sugar content while maltose may be found at levels three times higher than that of sucrose. The mineral fraction of honey is mainly composed of potassium and smaller amounts of magnesium, sodium, calcium, phosphorous, iron, manganese, cobalt and copper (Alves Da Silva *et al.*, 2006). Enzymes such as invertase, amylase, catalase and glucose oxidase are also present, and proline is the major amino acid constituent comprising about half the content of total free amino acids (White and Subers, 1963).

The beneficial role of honey is attributed to its antibacterial property with regards to its high osmolarity, acidity (low pH) and content of hydrogen peroxide (H_2O_2) and non-peroxide components, i.e., the presence of phytochemical components like methylglyoxal (MGO) (Weston, 2000; Mavric *et al.*, 2008). The antimicrobial agents in honey are predominantly hydrogen peroxide, of which the concentration is determined by relative levels of glucose oxidase, synthesized by the bee and catalase originating from flower pollen (Weston, 2000). Most types of honey generate H_2O_2 when diluted, because of the activation of the enzyme glucose oxidase that oxidizes glucose to gluconic acid and H_2O_2, which thus attributes the antimicrobial activity (Bang *et al.*, 2003). But, in some cases, the peroxide activity in honey can be destroyed easily by heat or the presence of catalase.

Besides H_2O_2, which was produced in most conventional honeys by the endogenous enzyme glucose oxidase, several other non-peroxide factors have been found to be responsible for the unique antibacterial activity of honey (Simon *et al.,* 2008). Honey may retain its antimicrobial activity even in the presence of catalase (absence of glucose oxidase), and thus this type of honey is regarded as "non-peroxide honey" (Molan, 1992; Simon, *et al.,* 2008). Several components are known to contribute the nonperoxide activity, such as the presence of methyl syringate and methylglyoxal, which have been extensively studied in manuka honey that is derived from the manuka tree (*L. scoparium*) (Adams *et al.*, 2008; Mavric *et al.*, 2008). Unlike manuka honey, the activity of ulmo honey is largely due to H_2O_2 production: 25 % (v/v) solution of ulmo honey had no detectable antibacterial activity when tested in presence of catalase. At the same concentration the manuka honey retained its antibacterial activity in the presence of catalase (absence of H_2O_2) (Sherlock *et al.*, 2010). Neither type of activity was influenced by the sterilizing procedure of gamma-irradiation (Simon *et al.*, 2008).

Citric and gluconic acids are also present in honey though malic, folic, lactic, succinic, butyric, acetic and formic acids have also been identified (Tan *et al.*, 1989). Honey, depending on variety, is a poor source of vitamins with only a few honeys showing evidence of vitamins A, B_2, C and B_6 and carotenoid- like substances (Alves Da Silva *et al.*, 2006). Polyphenols, especially flavonoids and phenolic acids are known to play an important role as antioxidants and honey is regarded as an important source of different compounds (Schramm *et al.*, 2003; Viuda Martos *et al.*, 2008). The presence and concentrations of these phytochemicals in honeys can vary depending upon the floral source, geographical and climatic conditions. Consequently, polyphenols have been suggested as floral markers for the botanical authentication of unifloral honeys (Amiot *et al.*, 1989; Jaganathan and Mandal, 2009).

Molan and Cooper (2000) reported that the difference in antimicrobial potency among the different honeys can be more than 100-fold, depending on its geographical, seasonal and botanical source as well as harvesting, processing and storage conditions. The antibacterial nature of honey was dependent on various factors working either singularly or synergistically, the most salient of which are H_2O_2, phenolic compounds, wound pH, pH of honey and osmotic pressure exerted by the honey. Hydrogen peroxide is the major contributor to the antimicrobial activity of honey, and the different concentrations of this compound in different honeys result in their varying antimicrobial effects (Molan, 1992). It has further been reported that physical property along with geographical distribution and different floral sources may play important role in the antimicrobial activity of honey (Taormina, 2001).

Several authors reported that different honeys vary substantially in the potency of their antibacterial activity, which varies with the plant source (Mundo *et al.*, 2004; Lusby *et al.*, 2005; Wilkinson and Cavanagh, 2005). Thus, it has been shown that the antimicrobial activity of honey may range from concentrations < 3 % to 50 % and higher (Lusby *et al.*, 2005; French *et al.*, 2005; Wilkinson and Cavanagh, 2005). The bactericidal effect of honey was reported to be dependent on concentration of honey used and the nature of the bacteria (Adeleke *et al.*, 2006; Basualdo *et al.*, 2007). The concentration of honey has an impact on antibacterial activity; the higher the concentration of honey the greater its usefulness as an antibacterial agent (Badawy *et al.*, 2004). Taormina *et al.* (2001) reported that the concentration of honey needed for complete inhibition of *Salmonella typhimurium* growth as <25 %.

Antimicrobial agents are essentially important in reducing the global burden of infectious diseases. However, as resistant pathogens develop and spread, the effectiveness of the antibiotics is diminished. This type of bacterial resistance to the antimicrobial agents poses a very serious threat to public health and for all kinds of antibiotics including the major last-resort drugs, the frequencies of resistance are increasing worldwide (Levy and Marshall, 2004; Mandal *et al.,* 2009). Therefore, alternative antimicrobial strategies are urgently needed and thus this situation has led to a re-evaluation of the therapeutic use of ancient remedies, such as plants and plant-based products, including honey (Basualdo *et al.,* 2007; Mandal *et al.,* 2010).

The use of traditional medicine to treat infection has been practiced since the origin of mankind and honey produced by *Apis mellifera* (*A. mellifera*) is one of the oldest traditional medicines considered to be important in the treatment of several human ailments. Currently, many researchers have reported the antibacterial activity of honey and found that natural unheated honey has some broad-spectrum antibacterial activity when tested against pathogenic bacteria, oral bacteria as well as food spoilage bacteria (Mundo *et al.,* 2004; Lusby *et al.,* 2005).

In most ancient cultures honey has been used for both domestic and medical purposes. The belief that honey is a nutrient, a drug and an ointment has been carried into our days and thus, an alternative medicine branch, called apitherapy, has been developed in recent years, offering treatments based on honey and other bee products against many diseases including bacterial infections. At present, a number of honeys are sold with standardized levels of antibacterial activity. The *Leptospermum scoparium* honey, the best known of the honeys has been reported to have an inhibitory effect on around 60 species of bacteria, including aerobes and anaerobes, Gram positives and Gram negatives (Molan, 1992).

Tan *et al.* (2009) reported that the Tualang honey was variable but broad-spectrum activities against many different kinds of wound and enteric bacteria. Unlike glucose oxidase, the antibacterial properties from *Leptospermum* spp. honeys are light and heat-stable. Natural honey of other sources can vary as much as 100-fold in the potency of their antibacterial activities which is due to hydrogen peroxide (Lusby *et al.,* 2005 51; French *et al.,* 2005 52). In addition, honey is hygroscopic which means that it can draw moisture out of the environment and dehydrate bacteria and its high sugar content and low level pH can also prevent the microbes from growth.

AIM OF THE PRESENT RESEARCH

To compare the antibacterial activity of natural and commercial honey against human pathogenic bacteria.

OBJECTIVES OF THE PRESENT RESEARCH

1) Collection of Natural and Commercial Honey samples.
2) Determination of antibacterial assay by Agar well diffusion method.

2. REVIEW OF LITERATURE

Microbial diseases are the major threat for the human health from the Stone Age to till now. The pathogenic activity of the microorganisms was mainly occurred due to the presence of a variety of virulence factors like capsule, endospore, antigens, polysaccharides, proteins, pili, enzymes and toxins. Among the various microorganisms in this universe, majority of the diseases are caused by bacteria and fungi. The microbial diseases are mainly transferred by three mechanisms *viz.*, Ingestion of water or food materials contaminated by microorganisms, Injection of microorganisms through insects or infected needles and Inhalation of microbial spores. In older days, the microbial infections are treated by Chemotherapy i.e., the method of treatment by using various chemicals. After the accidental discovery of the first Antibiotic Penicillin by Alexander Fleming from the mold *Penicillium notatum*, the use of chemotherapeutic agent was reduced and the peoples turned their eyes to Antibiotics. The antibiotics are the biological substance which was produced by the microorganisms which have the ability to kill or inhibit the growth of another microorganism. Based on its mode of action, antibiotics are classified into four categories *viz.*, Cell wall inhibitor, Cell membrane inhibitor, Protein synthesis inhibitor and Nucleic acid inhibitor. The first discovered antibiotic Penicillin is the Cell wall inhibitor.

After few years, the Penicillin becomes resistance to all the microorganisms and the scientists searched an alternative antibiotic for Penicillin. At the time, the great scientist who discovered more than ten antibiotics in his life time and named "Father of Antibiotics" has discovered the Protein synthesis inhibitor Streptomycin from the soil Actinobacteria *Streptomyces griseus*. The activity of Streptomycin is promising against various microbial disease and its usage was continued from previous years to present days. Nowadays, many antibiotics are commercially produced to treat various microbial diseases and it is playing an important role in the Pharmacological industry.

The antibiotic resistance has been in observed in present day against various microbial diseases due to its frequent usage. The antibiotic resistance was first observed in Penicillin against *Staphylococcus aureus* by the production of Beta – lactamase enzyme which degrades the Beta – lactum ring present in the Penicillin. But, nowadays the antibiotic resistance was extended against variety of antibiotics by many microorganisms. So, we are in need to find out an alternative medicine for treating various clinical microbial diseases caused by bacteria and fungi.

Traditional medicinal system is the method of using various natural products like seaweeds, plants and plant products for treating various diseases caused by microorganisms. The traditional medicinal system was used by the peoples in the older days but the entry of antibiotics has stopped the used of traditional medicines based treatment. The world rotation takes the peoples again to the traditional medicinal system due to the antibiotic resistance. The presence of bioactive compounds in the natural products gives an effective remedy against microbial diseases and prevents the humans from the risk of various side effects. On that line, the present study was designed to give the sweet remedy for microbial diseases using the Honey. The honey is an important part of traditional medicinal system which was used from older days to present days by all category of peoples.

The use of honey as a traditional medicine was quoted various thousands of years ago in various religious holy books like Holy Bible, Quran and Bhagavat Gita. The messenger of God, Prophet Mohammad Nabi (Peace been upon him) quoted honey as a "Healer of all diseases" Honey is a sugary syrup substance produced from the super saturated nectar, exudates of tree and secretions of plants flower by honey bees which belongs to the *Aphis* sp. it is also referred as an alimentary product of the *Aphis* sp. Biochemically, honey is composed of water and carbohydrate sugars with outstanding content of 31 % glucose and 38 % fructose and lesser content of 1 % sucrose. Honey is considered as a non-spoilage product due to the presence of mineral salts, vitamins and beneficial microorganisms. Other common ingredients of honey are amino acids (majorly proline), organic acids, hydrogen peroxide, enzymes, polyphenols, ascorbic acid, flavonoids, bee defensin, leptosin, methylglyoxal and phenolic acids. The mineral fractions available in the honey are iron, phosphorous, calcium, sodium, manganese, magnesium, copper, sodium and cobalt. Some pharmacologically important enzymes such as Glucose oxidase, Catalase, Amylase and Oxidase are present in honey (Alves Da Silva *et al.*, 2006; Saranraj *et al.*, 2016).

2.1. HISTORY OF HONEY AS MEDICINE

Honey is a popular sweetener throughout the world. According to an Associated Marketing survey conducted for the National Honey Board in 1997, almost 77 per cent of U.S. households use honey along with other sweeteners and syrups and 45 per cent of them consider honey a good value because it is "natural/good for you/better for you than sugar." Overall, honey has a positive profile with nearly 62 per cent of users "especially liking" it for its taste and flavor, 24 per cent because it is natural and 16 per cent because it is good for humans (Report on consumer uses and attitudes towards honey, 1997).

From ancient times, honey was not only used as a natural sweetener but also as a healing agent. Many health - promoting and curative properties attributed to it are the basis for some traditional folk medicine treatments throughout the world today. Of the consumers who use honey, 93 per cent consider honey a healthful product, recognizing it as a pure, natural product. Fifteen percent think of it as a good home remedy (Report on consumer uses and attitudes towards honey, 1997).

Stone age paintings in several locations dating to 6000 BC or earlier depict honey hunting, documenting human use of honey for at least 8000 years. References to honey as a medicine are found in ancient scrolls, tablets and books Sumerian clay tablets estimated to be 6200 BC, Egyptian papyri dated from 1900-1250 BC, Veda (Hindu scripture) about 5000 years old (Jones, 2001), the Holy Koran (Beck and Smedley, 1997), the Talmud, both the old and new testaments of the Bible, sacred books of India, China, Persia and Egypt and Hippocrates 460 - 357 BC. Clearly, honey was ubiquitous and our ancestors use of it for medicinal purposes was universal.

Honey was prescribed for a variety of uses including baldness, contraception and as a wound treatment. Frequently, honey was mixed with herbs, grains and other botanicals from the geographic area. Uses that have continued into modern folk medicine include treatment for coughs and sore throats, lotus honey for eye diseases in India, infected leg ulcers in Ghana, earaches in Nigeria, topical treatment of measles in the eyes to prevent corneal scarring, gastric ulcers and constipation (Molan, 2001).

2.2. NOMENCLATURE AND CLASSIFICATION OF HONEY

Honey is a saturated or supersaturated sugar solution produced by social bees and some other social insects. Bees and insects gather nectar or honeydew from the flower of living plants and process by the addition of enzymes into honey, then store as a food for use in dearth periods (Crane and Visscher, 2009). Despite the contributions of few other insects honey is chiefly produced by the bees which are social insects with a perennial life cycle. The bees are mainly classified into different groups which include all honey bees (*Apis spp.*), stingless bees (*Melipona* and *Trigona* spp.) as well as *Nectarina* wasps in South America and several species of honey ants, especially *Melophorus inflatus* in Australia. There are other social wasps and bumblebees (*Bombus* spp.) with annual life cycles which produce honey, but only very little (Crane, 1999).

2.2.1. Nectar Honey

The European Commission Council Directive 2001/110/CE (EU 110, 2001) defines nectar honey as natural sweet substance produced by *Apis mellifera* bees from the nectar of plants which the bees collect, transform by combining with specific substances of their own, deposit, dehydrate, store and leave in honeycombs to ripen and mature (EU 110, 2001).

2.2.2. Honeydew honey

European Commission Council Directive 2001/110/CE defines honeydew honey as a food obtained from secretions of living parts of plants or from excretions of plant-sucking insects. The plant-sucking insects (Hemiptera) pierce the foliage or other plant covering parts, feed on the sap, and excrete the surplus as droplets of honeydew, which are gathered by the bees (EU 110, 2001). Although, the differentiation of honeydew honeys and nectar honeys could be done by pollen analysis they are far better distinguished through their physicochemical profiles since the honeydew honeys have higher pH, acidity, ash, electrical conductivity, and darker colour, as well as lower monosaccharide and a higher di- and trisaccharide content (Mateo and Bosch-Reig, 1998). In addition, honeydew contains cells of algae and fungi; however, they are not specific for its origin (Bogdanov *et al.*, 1997).

2.3. COMPOSITION OF HONEY

2.3.1. Nutrients

Honey is a supersaturated sugar solution with approximately 17.1 per cent water. Fructose is the predominant sugar at 38.5 per cent, followed by glucose at 31 per cent. Disaccharides, trisaccharides and oligosaccharides were present in much smaller quantities. Besides carbohydrates, honey also contains small amounts of protein, (including enzymes), vitamins and minerals. Honey yields 64 calories per tablespoon, making it a more concentrated source of energy than other common sweeteners.

While the amino acid content is minor, the broad spectrum of approximately 18 essential and non - essential amino acids present in honey is unique and varies by floral source. Proline is the primary amino acid with lysine being the second most prevalent. Other amino acids found in honey included phenylalanine, tyrosine, glutamic and aspartic acids. The glutamic acid is a product of the glucose oxidase reaction.13 Proline and other amino acids were contributed by pollens, nectar or by the bees themselves (Crane, 1976).

Bees use a variety of plants to create honey and consequently, the nutritional profile of honey varies accordingly. Some studies have been done on honeys from different botanical origins to evaluate the differences in sugar content (Flodhazi, 1994), amino acid content (Pawlowska and Armstrong, 1994) and other components. These compositional differences can influence the value of a specific honey for medicinal or health-promoting purposes.

2.3.2. Phytochemicals

In recent years, researchers have identified a number of phytochemicals in various foods, including honey. Phytochemicals are the chemical substances which are present in plants. It is now recognized that many phytochemicals can have health - promoting activities. Antioxidants, a major group of phytochemicals, reduce the risk of tissue oxidative damage.

Honey is known to be rich in both enzymatic and non-enzymatic antioxidants, including catalase, ascorbic acid, flavonoids and alkaloids (Bogdanov,

1989; Berenbaum *et al.,* 1995; Berenbaum, 1996). A unique flavonoid, pinocembrin is present in high quantities in propolis and honey. Other flavonoids found in honey are pinobanksin, chrysin, galangin, quercetin, luteolin and kaempferol. Different honeys have different flavonoid profiles, depending on the floral source for the nectar. Similarly, the ascorbic acid content of honey ranges from 0.5 - 6.5 mg/100 g with an average of 2.4 mg/100 g or 5 mg/ml. However, some specific varieties of honey have been reported to contain as much as 75 - 150 mg ascorbic acid per 100 g, while most honey contain less than 5 mg/100 g (White, 1978).

In vitro experiments on the inhibition of oxidation in a model system using various honeys demonstrated a wide variation in the antioxidant capacity among floral sources. Honey made by bees fed herbal extracts exhibited greater antioxidant activity than normal honey (Rosenblat *et al.,* 1997). In general, higher antioxidant content was found in darker honeys and in honeys with higher water content (Frankel *et al.,* 1998). Some honeys such as buckwheat honey are comparable to fruits and vegetables such as orange pulp, broccoli and sweet peppers in their antioxidant content on a weight basis.

2.3.3. Enzymes

Honey contains a number of enzymes including glucose oxidase, invertase, diastase (amylase), catalase and acid phosphatase (Crane, 1976). The glucose oxidase reaction produces glutamic acid and hydrogen peroxide from glucose. It also produces glucolactone that equilibrates with gluconic acid. The hydrogen peroxide contributes to the antimicrobial properties of honey.

The invertase enzyme converts sucrose to fructose and glucose. It was added to the nectar by the bees as either gluco-invertase or fructo-invertase (Ensminger *et al.,* 1983). Some invertase is found in honey and may continue its activity in extracted honey. However, high temperatures will inactivate the invertase.

Diastase (amylase) splits starch chains to randomly produce dextrins and maltose (Crane, 1976). The diastase content varies according to floral source. Long storage periods and exposure to high temperatures for a prolonged period of time inactivate diastase. Researchers recommend 85 °C for 5 minutes to denature diastase in honey also a pH outside the optimum range of 5.3 - 5.6 will decrease diastase activity (Babacan *et al.,* 2002).

Catalase, found in small amounts in honey, produces oxygen and water from hydrogen peroxide. The inverse relationship between catalase activity and hydrogen peroxide content has been used to determine the hydrogen peroxide level of honey, formerly called the "inhibine number" (White *et al.,* 1963).

2.3.4. Organic acids

Organic acids contribute a slight tartness to the flavor of honey and add to its antimicrobial properties. Gluconic acid, the major organic acid, is the product of the enzymatic glucose oxidase reaction. It has been shown to increase calcium absorption (Fournier and Dupuis, 1975). Honey contains many other organic acids - butyric, acetic, formic, lactic, succinic, malic, citric, oxalic and pyroglutamic. The organic acid content varies according to the floral source (Stinson *et al.,* 1963).

2.4. MEDICINAL PROPERTIES OF HONEY

Honey is an ancient remedy for the treatment of infected wounds which has recently been 'rediscovered' by the medical profession, particularly where conventional modern therapeutic agents fail. The first written reference to honey, a Sumerian tablet writing, dating back to 2100 - 2000 BC, mentions honey's use as a drug and an ointment. Aristotle (384 - 322 BC), when discussing different honeys referred to pale honey as being "good as a salve for sore eyes and wounds". Manuka honey has been reported to exhibit antimicrobial activity against pathogenic bacteria such as *Staphylococcus aureus* and *Helicobacter pylori* making this honey a promising functional food for the treatment of wounds or stomach ulcers (French *et al.,* 2005).

The honey has been used from ancient times as a method of accelerating wound healing (Van Den Berg *et al.,* 2008), and the potential of honey to assist with wound healing has been demonstrated repeatedly (Molan, 2006; Simon *et al.,* 2008). Honey is gaining acceptance as an agent for the treatment of ulcers, bed sores and other skin infections resulting from burns and wounds (Cooper *et al.,* 2002). The healing properties of honey can be ascribed to the fact that it offers antibacterial activity, maintains a moist wound environment that promotes healing and has a high viscosity which helps to provide a protective barrier to prevent infection (Lusby *et al.,* 2005). There are many reports of honey being very effective as dressing of wounds, burns, skin ulcers and inflammations; the antibacterial properties of honey speed up the growth of new tissue to heal the wound (Lusby *et al.,* 2002). The med honey and manuka honey have been shown to have *in vivo* activity and are suitable for the treatment of ulcers, infected wounds and burns (Lusby *et al.,* 2005; Al-Waili *et al.,* 2005).

The honey when applied topically, rapidly clears wound infection to facilitate healing of deep surgical wounds with infection (Ahmed *et al.,* 2003). The application of honey can promote the healing in infected wounds that do not respond to the conventional therapy, i.e., antibiotics and antiseptics (Ahmed *et al.,* 2003), including wounds infected with Methicillin - resistant *Staphylococcus aureus* (Natarajan *et al.,* 2001). Moreover, it can be used on skin grafts and infected skin graft donor sites successfully (Misirlioglu *et al.,* 2003).

The manuka, jelly bush and pasture honeys are capable of stimulating the monocytes, the precursors of macrophages, to secrete TNF-α (Tonks *et al.,* 2003). On the other hand, glycosylated proteins can induce TNF-α secretion by macrophages and this cytokine is known to induce the mechanism of wound repairing. Furthermore, the ability of honey to reduce 'reactive intermediates release (Tonks *et al.,* 2001) may well limit tissue damage by activated macrophages during wound healing. Thus, the immune modulatory property of honey is relevant to wound repair.

The support for using honey as a treatment regimen for peptic ulcers and gastritis comes from traditional folklore as well as from reports in modern times (Molan, 2001). Honey may promote the repair of damaged intestinal mucosa, stimulate the growth of new tissues and work as an antiinflammatory agent (Molan, 2001). Raw honey contains copious amounts of compounds such as flavonoids and other polyphenols which may function as antioxidants (Blassa *et al.,* 2006). Clinical observations have been reported of reduced symptoms of inflammation when honey is applied to wounds. The removal of exudates in wounds dressed with honey is of help in managing inflamed wounds (Ahmed *et al.,* 2003).

2.5. ANTIMICROBIAL ACTIVITY OF HONEY

2.5.1. Mechanisms of antimicrobial activity

A number of characteristics of honey contribute to its antimicrobial activity. The enzymatic glucose oxidation reaction and some of its physical properties are considered to be the major factors. Other factors include high osmotic pressure/low water activity (A_w), low pH/acidic environment, low protein content, high carbon to nitrogen ratio, low redox potential due to the high content of reducing sugars; a viscosity that limits dissolved oxygen and other chemical agents/ phytochemicals (Snowden and Cliver, 1996). The most familiar Honey researcher, Dr. Peter Molan has written an extensive review of the research on the antimicrobial factors in honey and has summarized the key aspects of his research on a website at the University of Waikato, Hamilton, New Zealand.

- Honey is a supersaturated sugar solution with a low water activity (A_w), which means that there is little water available to support the growth of bacteria and yeast. Many species of bacteria will grow if the A_w is between 0.94 - 0.99 and the A_w of ripened honey (0.56 - 0.62) does not support the growth of yeast. Diluted honey with a higher A_w will not be effective against those species of bacteria that grow most rapidly at an A_w of 0.99.
- The natural acidity of honey will inhibit many pathogens. The minimum pH value for some species that commonly infect wounds ranges from 4.0 - 4.5. Dilution of honey, especially with body fluids will raise the pH and lessen the antibacterial effectiveness that results from its acidity.
- Glucose oxidase is an enzyme secreted by the bees to form honey from nectar. It converts glucose in the presence of water and oxygen to gluconic acid and hydrogen peroxide. The resulting acidity and hydrogen peroxide preserve and sterilize the honey during the ripening process. Full-strength honey has negligible amounts of hydrogen peroxide and active glucose oxidase. Transition ions and ascorbic acids rapidly decompose hydrogen peroxide to oxygen and water while the low pH inactivates the enzyme. However, dilution of honey results in a 2,500 - 50,000 increase in enzyme activity and a "slow-release" antiseptic that does not damage tissue.
- The peroxide-generating system does not account for all of the observed antibacterial activity. Several substances with antibacterial activity were found in honey in small quantities that are too low to contribute significantly to antibacterial activity: pinocembrin, terpenes, benzyl alcohol, 3,5- dimethoxy-4-hydroxybenzoic acid (syringic acid), methyl-3,5-dimethoxy-4-hydroxybenzoate (methyl syringate), 3,4,5-trimethoxybenzoic acid, 2-hydroxy-3-phenylpropionic acid, 2-hydroxybenzoic acid and 1,4-dihydroxybenzene. Support for the existence of non-peroxide antimicrobial factors comes from reports of continued activity after honey has been treated

with heat, thereby inactivating the glucose oxidase, and after honey has been treated with catalase to remove the peroxide activity.

Not all honeys are created equal in antimicrobial activity due to differences in levels of peroxide production and non-peroxide factors, which vary by floral source and processing. The presence of metal ions, ascorbic acid and catalase from the nectar can destroy the hydrogen peroxide. Heat and light can destroy the glucose oxidase enzyme. The original method for measuring antibacterial activity was to determine the "inhibine number" defined as the degree of dilution (done in a stepwise fashion) to which a honey will retain its antibacterial activity. Most studies now report antimicrobial activity as minimum inhibitory concentration (MIC), the minimum concentration necessary for complete inhibition of growth (Molan, 2002). Various studies on large numbers of honey samples showed a wide range of activity and many with only a low level of activity (Allen *et al.*, 1991).

While there are insufficient data to clearly identify the antibacterial activity of all honeys, there is some evidence of high levels in honeydew honey (a sweet liquid excreted by sucking insects which tap into leaves) from the conifer forests of the mountainous regions of central Europe and manuka honey (honey from the *Leptospermum* species) from New Zealand. Honey had the highest levels of non-peroxide activity among 26 different types of honey from various floral sources. It strongly inhibited two strains of bacteria (*Escherichia coli* and *Staphylococcus aureus*) (Willix *et al.,* 1992).

An *in vitro* study compared the antibacterial action of a pasture honey (a polyfloral honey in which the nectar comes from various clovers and pasture weeds such as thistle and dandelion) and manuka honey on coagulase positive *Staphylococcus aureus* strains from infected wounds. The isolates showed little difference in their sensitivity to both honeys. The pasture honey with a higher peroxide generation and the manuka honey with non - peroxidal antibacterial activity were both effective at low concentrations (3 - 4 percent v/v and 2 - 3 per cent v/v, respectively) (Cooper *et al.,* 1999).

2.5.2. Antibacterial activity

There are several studies investigating the antimicrobial activity of honey. The antibacterial activity of honey is usually associated with the release of hydrogen peroxide, from the oxidation of glucose to glucolactone and then to gluconic acid in presence of the enzyme glucose oxidase. This activity was called peroxide-activity and constitutes, at variable extent, the mode of action of some honeys (Henriques *et al.,* 2006). The use of honey as a traditional remedy for microbial infections dates back to ancient times.

Research has been conducted on manuka (*L. scoparium*) honey (Visavadia *et al.,* 2006), which has been demonstrated to be effective against several human pathogens, including *Escherichia coli, Enterobacter aerogenes, Salmonella typhimurium, Staphylococcus aureus* (Lusby *et al.,* 2005; Visavadia *et al.,* 2006). Many laboratory studies have revealed that the honey is effective against Methicillin-resistant *Staphylococcus aureus* (MRSA), β- haemolytic *Streptococci* and vancomycin resistant *Enterococci* (VRE) (Allen *et al.,* 2000 96; Kingsley, 2001 97). However, the newly identified honeys may have advantages over or similarities with manuka honey due to enhanced antimicrobial activity, local production (thus availability) and greater selectivity against medically important organisms (Lusby *et al.,* 2005). The coagulase negative *Staphylococci* are very similar to *Staphylococcus aureus* (Cooper *et al.,* 2002; Abhishek *et al.,* 2010) in their susceptibility to honey of similar antibacterial potency and more susceptible than *Pseudomonas aeruginosa* and *Enterococcus* species (Cooper *et al.,* 2002).

Gram positive bacteria such as *Staphylococcus aureus,* the causal agent of a range of illnesses from skin infections to life-threatening diseases such as pneumonia and meningitis, did not grow in the presence of honeys produced by *A. mellifera* and *Tetragonisca angustula* bees in the Brazilian states of Paraná and Minas Gerais. In order to study this effect, honeys were analysed by high performance liquid chormatography (HPLC) and the antimicrobial activity was connected to phenolic compounds, such as 4- hydroxybenzoic acid (HBEN). These compounds occur in higher concentrations in propolis than in honey and propolis was more effective against *Staphylococcus aureus* than honey (Miorin *et al.,* 2003). This bacterium has proved to be variable in susceptibility to different honeys. Turkish honeys from Anatolia showed a moderate inhibition towards some strains of *Staphylococcus aureus* (Kucuk *et al.,* 2007), while Turkish rhododendron honeys partially inhibited the growth of this bacterium (Silici *et al.,* 2010).

Honey from stingless bees had powerful activity against *Staphylococcus aureus* when compared to that exhibited by manuka honey produced by honeybees belonging to Apidae family (*A. mellifera, A. cerana*) (Temaru *et al.*, 2007). Argentinean honeys from the province of Cordoba evidenced high activity against *Staphylococcus aureus,* which was considered to be of remarkable clinical importance, since an increase in difficult-to-treat skin infections had been reported in the last decade and resistance against several antibiotics had developed (Basualdo *et al.*, 2007). A study of the properties of several Cuban honeys demonstrated that Gram positive bacteria are more sensitive than Gram negative bacteria with *Staphylococcus aureus* the most sensitive bacterium (Alvarez Suarez *et al.*, 2010).

Honeys from *A. mellifera* produced in Thailand also showed inhibitory effects against many infectious diseases (Srisayam and Chantawannakul, 2010). Strains of *Staphylococcus aureus* were found to be very sensitive to Spanish honeydew honeys (Perez Martin *et al.*, 2008) whereas in other studies using honeys from Galicia (northwest of Spain) two strains of the bacterium, including a difficult-to-treat strain in humans such as the methicillin-resistant *Staphylococcus aureus* (MRSA), exhibited different sensitivities (Gallardo - Chacon *et al.*, 2008). South African honeys from indigenous *Leucospermum cordifolium* and *Erica* species showed poor antibacterial activity against this Gram positive bacterium (Basson and Grobler, 2008).

Basualdo *et al.* (2007) demonstrated that *Escherichia coli* can be inhibited by some Argentinean honeys while, Fangio *et al.* (2010) demonstrated the effectiveness of honeys produced in the province of Buenos Aires (Argentina) against this *Enterobacter* sp. The antimicrobial activity of these honeys was mainly non-peroxide and the presence of phytochemicals such as phenolic compounds was considered in the most active honeys. Nevertheless, rhododendron Turkish honeys showed no inhibitory effect (Silici *et al.*, 2010).

Baltrusaityte *et al.* (2007) observed that Lithuanian honeys exhibited antibacterial effects on *Staphylococcus aureus* and concluded that this was mainly due to the presence of hydrogen peroxide. Honeys produced in the Czech Republic are also antimicrobially effective with some honeydew honeys possessing the greatest effects (Vorlova *et al.*, 2005). In a study with unifloral and multifloral Portuguese honeys, Henriques *et al.* (2005) analyzed their antibacterial activity against a strain of *Staphylococcus aureus*, and observed that all of the samples tested possessed peroxide activity except some honeys derived from *Lavandula stoechas* which revealed non - peroxide antibacterial activity.

Basson and Grobler (2008) found poor antibiotic activity of South African honeys from indigenous *L. cordifolium* and *Erica* species. Some Czech Republican honeys were also tested for their antibacterial activity against *Escherichia coli* and researchers concluded that honeydew honeys are the most effective (Vorlova *et al.*, 2005). Recently, Brudzynski and Miotto (2011) investigation with twenty Canadian unheated honeys, quantified Maillard reaction - like products (MRLPs) and total phenol contents, apart from assessing the antioxidant activity using the ORAC method. One of their results indicated that both the recorded antioxidant activity and the content of MRLPs of these honeys mainly contributed to the antibacterial activity against *Escherichia coli*. This antibacterial activity confirms the work of Rufian Henares and De La Cueva (2009) who suggested that the antibacterial activity of coffee melanoidins against *Escherichia coli* is due to their behavior as metalchelators.

Isla *et al.* (2011) observed that algarrobo honey (*Prosopis nigra*) and a multifloral honey from the northwestern provinces of Argentina had activity against *Staphylococcus aureus.* They identified at least five antibacterial compounds in the algarrobo honey and four compounds in the multifloral honey and found that most of them corresponded to flavonoids. One of these flavonoids was identified as pinocembrin. The authors also pointed out that the antibacterial activity of the analysed honeys might be mainly due to their phenol content because of the significant correlation observed between the phenolic content and the antibacterial activity.

Among the Gram negative bacteria, *Escherichia coli* is of great concern from a health point of view. It may cause life threatening gastric infections and diarrhoea, following consumption of contaminated food, as well as other infections such as cystitis, meningitis, peritonitis and pneumonia. There are several studies on the antibiotic effect of honey towards *Escherichia coli.* The *Escherichia coli* exhibited sensitivity to stingless honeybee honey (Temaru *et al.*, 2007), Spanish honeys (Gallardo - Chacon *et al.*, 2008), Cuban honeys (Alvarez - Suarez *et al.*, 2010), and Thailand honeys (Srisayam and Chantawanakul, 2010).

Pseudomonas aeruginosa, an important pathogenic bacterium which can cause several health disorders in humans including lung, urinary, tissue, blood and wound infections was studied in many published reports. Silici *et al.* (2010) showed that rhododendron honeys from Turkey have antimicrobial activity against *Pseudomonas aeruginosa* when diluted at 50 % and 75 % in water. *A. mellifera* honeys produced in Thailand also inhibited the growth of this bacterium (Srisayam and Chantawannakul, 2010). Honey from stingless honeybees showed significant inhibitory effects on the growth of *Pseudomonas aeruginosa* (Temaru *et al.*, 2007). The bactericidal potency of Saharan honey against this pathogen was studied by Boukraa and Niar (2007) who reported that Saharan honey showed higher potency than Algerian honeys, probably due to antibacterial substances from the botanic flora occurring in the Sahara. This Gram negative and aerobic microorganism was sensitive to some honeys produced in the province of Córdoba (Argentina) (Basualdo *et al.*, 2007), but was the least sensitive in comparison with other bacteria (Alvarez-Suarez *et al.*, 2010), while not sensitive to honey samples evaluated by Gallardo - Chacon *et al.* (2008).

Helicobacter pylori, can occur in the stomach, and is linked to the development of ulcers and many types of gastritis. There is evidence that honey can have inhibitory effects against this bacterium. Kucuk *et al.* (2007) reported a moderate inhibitory effect by honeys harvested in Anatolia (Turkey), and studies conducted with manuka (*L. scoparium*) honey showed interesting antibacterial activity (Mavric *et al.*, 2008; Adams *et al.*, 2008; Attrot and Henle, 2009). It has been suggested that this honey can also act by healing the gastric mucosa and stimulating epithelial cells growth.

Bacillus cereus, a Gram positive, aerobic and beta - hemolytic bacterium is a food-borne pathogen for humans whose growth results in the production of enterotoxins causing nausea, vomiting, abdominal cramps and diarrhoea. There are reports of the sensitivity of the bacterium towards some honeys. For example, some Thai honeys can inhibit growth of the *Bacillus* (Srisayam and Chantawannakul, 2010) and similar activity was observed in studies using different honeys which included honey from Galicia (Spain) (Gallardo - Chacon *et al.*, 2008). In contrast, *Bacillus cereus* was found to be resistant when rhododendron Turkish honeys were tested for their antibacterial activity (Silici *et al.*, 2010).

Honeys produced in Anatolia (Turkey) in Cuba and in the Turkish Black Sea Region showed inhibition effects on strains of *Bacillus subtilis* (Kucuk *et al.*, 2007; Silici *et al.*, 2010; Alvarez-Suarez *et al.*, 2010), a Gram positive sporing bacterium occurring in soil which can contaminate food but rarely causes infections in humans.

Some other honey sensitive - pathogens described in the literature are *Bacillus anthrasis* (anthrax), *Corynebacterium diptheriae* (diphtheria), *Klebsiella pneumoniae* (pneumonia), *Mycobacterium tuberculosis* (tuberculosis), *Salmonella typhi* (typhoid fever), *Vibrio cholerae* (cholera) and different *Streptococci,* among others. For example, *Klebsiella pneumoniae* was found to be sensitive to Argentinean (Basualdo *et al.*, 2007), and Thai honeys (Srisayam and Chantawannakul, 2010). The growth of *Enterococcus faecalis* was inhibited by stingless honeybee honey (Temaru *et al.*, 2007) and this bacterium also showed sensitivity to honey according to the research performed by Gallardo - Chacon *et al.* (2008).

In addition, other bacteria sensitive to different types of honey are *Staphylococcus epidermidis* (Basualdo *et al.*, 2007; Baltrusaityte, 2007), *Staphylococcus uberis* (Basualdo *et al.*, 2007), *Pediococcus mirabilis* (Silici *et al.*, 2010), *Aeromonas hydrophila* (Silici *et al.*, 2010), *Micrococcus luteus* (Srisayam and Chantawannakul, 2010), *Streptococcus oralis* (Basson and Grobler, 2008), *Streptococcus anginosus* (Basson and Grobler, 2008), *Salmonella enterica* ser. *typhimurium* (Vorlova *et al.*, 2005; Gallardo Chacón *et al.*, 2008), *Shigella sonnei* (Gallardo Chacon *et al.*, 2008), *Listeria monocytogenes* (Vorlova *et al.*, 2005; Gallardo Chacon *et al.*, 2008) and *Streptococcus mutans* (Basson and Grobler, 2008). Among yeasts, some *Candida* species were inhibited by Turkish honeys (Kucuk *et al.*, 2007).

The initial event in the development of bacterial infections of the gastrointestinal gut is the attachment of bacteria to the mucosal epithelial cells (Raupach *et al.*, 1999) and the blocking of this event represents an interesting strategy for the prevention of diseases (O'Farrelly *et al.*, 1992; Peralta *et al.*, 1994). Alnaqdy *et al.* (2005) studied the antimicrobial activity of Omani honeys against *Salmonella interitidis* and the ability of these honeys to prevent the bacterium from adhering to intestinal epithelial cells *in vitro*. However, in spite of the antimicrobial activity, there are yeasts like *Candida albicans* and *Saccharomyces cerevisiae* which showed resistance towards some honeys (Silici *et al.*, 2010; Srisayam and Chantawannakul, 2010), while rhododendron honeys were not effective against strains of *Bacillus cereus, Escherichia coli* and *Yersinia enterocolitica* (Silici *et al.*, 2010).

The bactericidal properties of honey led researchers to investigate its applications on cutaneous wound healing and the treatment of burns. Mohd Nasir *et al.* (2010) and Kirnpal Kaur *et al.* (2011) found that Tualang honey (*Koompassia excelsa*) had important bactericidal and bacteriostatic effects in the treatment of burns by using dressings soaked with this honey. Also, non - toxicity of honey against tissue cell cultures of human keratinocyte and fibroblasts has recently been found *in vitro.* This kind of evidence may positively influence the choice of wound dressings in clinical prescriptions (Du Toit and Page, 2009).

2.5.3. Antiviral activity of Honey

Antiviral properties of honeys are also of great concern from a therapeutic point of view. Chritchfield *et al.* (1995) showed that some important flavonoids of honey such as chrysin, acacetin andapigenin can inhibit the Human immunodeficiency virus (HIV-1) activation *via* a probable mechanism involving the inhibition of viral transcription. Other researchers have demonstrated the inhibitory effects of chrysin against herpes simplex virus type 1 (HSV-1) (Lyu *et al.*, 2005). Hu *et al.* (1994) observed that chrysin and apigenin have a significant antiviral activity against HIV-1 in acutely infected H9 lymphocytes. Apigenin also exhibited antiviral activity against influenza virus (H3N2) *in vitro* (Liu *et al.*, 2008).

Molecular biological processes at DNA level are responsible for cell events that lead to the development of some phenomena such as carcinogenesis, and, in this line, binding studies of different flavonoids were undertaken. Apigenin, a cancer chemopreventive agent, has the highest affinity of ligand-DNA binding when compared to those of morine and naringin (Nafisi *et al.*, 2008).

Al - Waili (2004) studied the activity of honey on two types of herpes: labial and genital herpes. His results demonstrated that the topic application of honey on recurrent attacks of this viral disease was effective. This study reported that in the labial herpes the mean time of healing was 43 % better than with the conventional treatment with acyclovir, while for genital herpes the mean healing time was improved around 59 %. The authors remarked that some cases remitted completely after treatment with honey, although none of the attack remitted when using acyclovir. Honey has also demonstrated anti-Rubella activity in experiments performed on monkey kidney cell cultures infected with the Rubella virus (Zeina *et al.*, 1996).

Chiang *et al.* (2005) observed that apigenin behaves as a potent antiviral substance against Herpes virus type - 2 (HSV-2), Adenovirus (ADV-3), Hepatitis B surface antigen (HDCA) and Hepatitis B e antigen (HBeA).

2.6. HONEY APPLICATIONS – A HISTORICAL PRESPECTIVES

Honey has been a valuable food, medicine and sweetener throughout the ages. Although it is difficult to follow exactly when the relationship between humans and the bees started and all the efforts by which ancient people have tried to domesticate the bees and how exactly humans have learned to get the best out of them this section summarizes some of the literature citing the uses of honey.

2.6.1. Honey in Ancient times

The use of honey for therapeutical purposes is well established in ancient prescriptions as well as modern wound management. The earliest records of the application of honey in medicine could be traced back to the Egyptian Papyri as well as Sumerian clay tablets dated from 1900 to 1250 BC where honey was in almost one third of the prescriptions (Molan, 1992). Other uses of honey by ancient Egyptians also included treatments for the eyes and skin as well as in embalming and wounds. "Hippocrates (460-357 BC) found that honey cleaned sores and ulcers of the lips and healed buncles and running sores. Aristotle (384-322 BC) referred to pale honey being a good salve for sore eyes" (Al Waili, 2003). The ancient Greeks were reported to have used honey to treat fatigue: athletes drank a mixture of honey and water before major athletic events (Crane, 1975).

The Babylonian used honey for the treatment of ear infections, eye infections and an ointment for the skin (Henriques, 2006). The medicinal uses of honey alone and in combination with other components including herbs and essential oils to treat various ailments including burns, wounds, eye infections as well as gastrointestinal disorders might be traced back to ancient civilizations of the Egyptians, Assyrians, Greeks and Romans (Zumla and Lulat, 1989). In 50 AD, Dioscorides described honey as being "good for all rotten and hollow ulcers" and "good for sunburn and spots on the face" (Molan, 2006). Many African tribes use honey to treat snakebites, fever and as a laxative. Moreover, the Masai warriors have used honey to gain more power and enhance their strength which is probably due to the high sugar content of honey (Henriques, 2006).

It has been reported that the Egyptians used honey in their spiced breads, cakes and pastries, and for priming beer and wine (Tannahill, 1975). In Ancient Rome honey was used in a wider range of culinary dishes. Honey has been used in salad dressings in order to balance the acidity of the vinegar as well as an essential ingredient of many sauces (Crane, 1975). Reports have mentioned that the wines drunk at the beginning and end of meals were sweetened with honey; and meat, while fruit and vegetables were sometimes preserved by immersion in honey (Free, 1982). Refined sugar which is used in cooking today has been known and used in medicines, but had no place in cooking (Wilson, 1973). Almost half of one late Roman cookery book included honey as an ingredient in almost 500 recipes (Style, 1992).

2.6.2. Honey use in Middle ages

During the Middle Ages honey was used for sweetening all type of dishes from appetizers, soups, cheese to fish dishes, roast meats as well as vegetables. However, it is difficult to predict whether a dish is savoury or sweet from the title assigned to it in a recipe. Today it is easy to predict a meat or cheese dish will usually be savoury; however, it was not the same in the Middle Ages, where meat, fish dishes and the pastry lids of 'savoury' pies might often be sweetened (Wilson, 1973).

Daude de Pradas has reported the application of honey in folk medicine in approximately 1200 AD (Crane, 1975). In a text book about honey Beck and Smedley (1997) have mentioned that honey has been used as a remedy for gastric and intestinal complaints, the diuretic effect of honey were recorded as a favoured remedy for kidney inflammations and stones. In addition Hindu people had great faith in the medical virtues of honey, mainly for the treatment of coughs, pulmonary issues and gastric disorders. Moreover, they have reported the use of particular honeys for the treatment of specific disorders and the general application of honeys for treatment of skin diseases and smallpox, as well as in surgical dressings. Furthermore, they also reported the use of a mixture of honey and crushed bees by German women for the regulation of the menstrual flow as well as the energetic and cosmetic benefits (Beck and Smedley, 1997).

2.6.3. Honey in Modern medicine

In more recent times, honey has played a relatively minor role in medicine in the developed countries mostly due to it not being accepted by Western practitioners who preferred to use to antibiotics since they were not sure of the honeys' mode of action (Molan, 1992a). However; the applications of honey continued in the Middle East, China, Africa and Indian nations since they consider honey as a valuable source for the treatment of internal as well as external ailments (Beck and Smedley, 1997).

Populations in rural communities from almost all nations have documented the use of honey for wounds management as well as other ailments through time (Henriques *et al.,* 2010). Honey has been shown in one clinical trial to be effective against bacterial diarrhoea, (Haffejee and Moosa, 1985), and to aid in the treatment of eye infections (Molan, 2001; Al Waili, 2004). Although, honey has played a minor role in Western medicine since the development of Penicillin and other antibiotics which were considered as miracle drugs they were forced to rediscover the antibacterial potential of honeys; probably due to the emergence of multi-drug resistant pathogens such as methicillin resistant *Staphylococcus aureus* (MRSA), vancomycin resistant enterococci (VRE) and *Pseudomonas aeruginosa* (Molan, 1992).

Throughout the last two decades much research has been carried out in order to explore the mysterious role played by honey in the management of wounds and burns, which has led to scientific evidence that demonstrated honey is an effective antibacterial agent (Molan and Allen, 1996; Cooper *et al.*, 2002). The *in vitro* findings that honey is an effective antibacterial agent and proved to be even superior to many antiseptics and antibiotics are matching with the clinical trials as well as the *in vivo* and in vitro experiments that was demonstrated by many cases in which honey successfully eradicated antibiotic resistant and sensitive strains that conventional therapy has failed to eradicate (Subrahmanyam, 1991).

Medicinally, honey is used to enhance wound- healing in humans (Aysan *et al.*, 2002), treatment of gastric ulcer (Kandil *et al.,* 1987) and shortening of the duration of diarrhoea (Haffejee and Moosa, 1985). The use of honey was based on empirical knowledge rather than scientific knowledge. People didn't know how honeys cured infections but, knew it worked, this fact led to the use of antibiotics instead of honey (Molan, 2001).

Only now researchers are beginning to understand why honey has such therapeutic and beneficial potential; honey indeed could be the elixir (Molan and Allen, 1996) that the ancient people believed. Research is showing a number of other health-related benefits, including a laxative effect, beneficial effects on blood glucose levels (Cortes *et al.,* 2011), anti-inflammatory and immune stimulating properties and potentially a cancer-preventative action (Manyi-Loh *et al.,* 2011).

2.7. USES OF HONEY

The use of honey as a traditional remedy for microbial infections dates back to ancient times. The ability of honey to kill microorganisms has been attributed to its high osmotic effect, high acidic nature, hydrogen peroxide concentration and its phytochemical nature (Molan, 2000).

2.7.1. Therapeutic uses

In most cases, honey is used when conventional antibacterial treatment with antibiotics and antiseptics are ineffective. Numerous studies have shown that these difficult-to-heal wounds respond well to honey dressings. Inflammation, swelling and pain rapidly subside, unpleasant odours stop, debridement is enhanced as the honey dressings remove dead tissue painlessly and without causing damage to the regrowing cells. Honey promotes rapid healing with minimal scarring. Honey can also be used as first aid treatment for burns as it has potent anti-inflammatory activity

2.7.2. Medicinal Properties

Recent tests carried out in collaboration with the Central Public Health Laboratory in London, UK, on many strains of multi-antibiotic resistant bacteria such as MRSA strains MRSA, VRE and *Acinetobacter baumarii* have shown that these bacteria have no resistance to honey (These "superbugs" are a serious clinical problem as infections with them often cannot be treated at all with antibiotics). All of the testing of sensitivity of wound infecting species of bacteria that we have carried out has been done with honeys selected to have mid-range levels of antibacterial activity.

Another important factor for growth of new tissue is a supply of nutrients, usually limited because of damage to the underlying circulation resulting from injury or infection. Honey will supply the cells with a wide range of vitamins, amino acids and minerals. It will also supply white blood cells with the glucose necessary for their "respiratory burst" to destroy bacteria. Further, it will supply nutrients to the cells by drawing serum out through the tissue by osmosis induced by the high sugar content of honey

2.7.3. Honey as Antibiotic

Manuka honey has potent antibacterial properties, making it especially beneficial for preventing and treating wound infections by drug-resistant bacteria, according to physician Robert Frykberg of the Veterans Affairs Medical Center in Phoenix, Ariz.

2.7.4. Diabetic Benefits

FDA-approved Manuka honey product, Medi honey, has proven beneficial for healing foot ulcers in diabetic patients. Diabetics with foot ulcers that do not heal sometimes require foot amputation.

2.7.5. Gastrointestinal Effects

Manuka honey shows promise for healing peptic ulcers caused by *Helicobacter pylori* bacteria, in research cited by the University of Waikato in New Zealand. It is also effective against various strains of bacteria that cause gastroenteritis.

2.7.6. Recent Medicinal Research on Honey

For centuries honey had been known as nature's medicine. Ongoing medical research is turning up a multitude of curative uses for honey. Medicinal benefits and uses of honey as a natural remedy. Honey is not only for eating, but has several different medicinal uses

2.7.7. Arthritis

Take one part honey to two parts of luke warm water and add a small teaspoon of cinnamon powder, make a paste and massage it on the itching part of the body. It was noticed that the pain recedes within a minute. For arthritis, patients daily morning and night take one cup of hot water with two spoons of honey and one small teaspoon of cinnamon powder. If drunk regularly even chronic arthritis can be cured. In a recent research done at the Coppenhagen University, it was found that when the doctors treated their patients with a mixture of one tablespoon honey and half teaspoon cinnamon powder before breakfast, they found that within a week out of the 200 people so treated practically 73 patients were totally relieved of pain and within a month, mostly all the who could not walk or move around because of arthritis started walking without pain.

2.7.8. Bladder infections

Take two tablespoons of cinnamon powder and one teaspoon of honey in a glass of luke warm water and drink it. It destroys the germs of the bladder.

2.7.9. Cholesterol

Two tablespoons of honey and three teaspoons of cinnamon powder mixed in 16 ounces of tea water if given to a cholesterol patient; it reduces the level of cholesterol in the body by 10% within 2 hours. As mentioned for arthritic patients, if taken 3 times a day any chronic cholesterol cured. As per the information received in the said journal, pure honey taken with food daily relieves complains of cholesterol.

2.7.10. Upset stomach

Honey taken with cinnamon powder cures stomachache and also clears stomach ulcers from the root. Gas: according to the studies done in India & Japan. It was revealed that if honey is taken with cinnamon powder the stomach is relieved of gas.

2.7.11. Immune system

Daily use of honey and cinnamon powder strengthens the immune system and protects the body from bacterial and viral attacks. Scientists have found that honey has various vitamins and iron in large amounts. Constants use of honey strengthens the white blood corpuscles to fight bacterial and viral diseases.

2.7.12. Influenza

A scientist in Spain has proved that honey contains a natural ingredient, which kills the influenza germs and saves the patient from flu.

2.7.13. Skin infections

Applying honey and cinnamon powder in equal parts on the affected parts cures eczema, ringworm and all types of skin infections.

2.7.14. Cancer

Recent research in Japan and Australia has revealed that advanced cancer of the stomach and bones have been cured successfully. Patients suffering from these kinds ofcancer should daily take one tablespoon of honey with one teaspoon of cinnamon powder for one month 3 times a day.

2.7.15. Wound Healing

Honey is one of the oldest known medicines that have continued to be used up to present times in folk - medicine. Its use has been "rediscovered" in later times by the medical profession, especially for dressing wounds. The numerous reports of the effectiveness of honey in wound management, including reports of several randomized controlled trials, have recently been reviewed, rapid clearance of infection from the treated wounds being a commonly recorded observation. In almost all of these reports, honey was referred to generically, there being no indication given of any awareness of the variability that generally is found in natural products.

Any honey can be expected to suppress infection in wounds because of its high sugar content, but dressings of sugar on a wound have to be changed more frequently than honey dressings do to maintain an osmolarity that is inhibitory to bacteria, as honey has additional antibacterial components. Since, microbiological studies have shown more than one hundred - fold differences in the potency of the antibacterial activity of various honey, best results would be expected if a honey with a high level of antibacterial activity were used in the management of infected wounds (Sampath Kumar, 2010).

2.8. OTHER MEDICINAL USES OF HONEY

2.8.1. Honey as Antibiotics

Manuka honey has potent antibacterial properties, making it especially beneficial for preventing and treating wound infections by drug-resistant bacteria, according to physician Robert Frykberg of the Veterans Affairs Medical Center in Phoenix, Ariz.

2.8.2. Antidiabetic activity

Frykberg noted that the FDA-approved manuka honey product, Medihoney, has proven beneficial for healing foot ulcers in diabetic patients. Diabetics with foot ulcers that do not heal sometimes require foot amputation.

2.8.3. Arthritis

Take one part honey to two parts of luke warm water and add a small teaspoon of cinnamon powder, make a paste and massage it on the itching part of the body. It is noticed that the pain recedes within a minute or two. Or for arthritis patients daily morning and night take one cup of hot water with two spoons of honey and one small teaspoon of cinnamon powder. If drunk regularly even chronic arthritis can be cured. In a recent research done at the Coppen Hagen University, it was found that when the doctors treated their patients with a mixture of one tablespoon honey and half teaspoon cinnamon powder before breakfast, they found that within a week out of the 200 people so treated practically 73 patients were totally relieved of pain and within a month, mostly all the patients who could not walk or move around because of arthritis started walking without pain.

2.8.4. Hair Loss

Those suffering from hair loss or baldness may apply a paste of hot olive oil, one tablespoon or honey, one teaspoon cinnamon powder before bath and keep it for approximately 15 min. And then wash the hair. It was found very effective even if kept for 5 min.

2.8.5. Bladder Infections

Take two tablespoons of cinnamon powder and one teaspoon of honey in a glass of luke warm water and drink it. It destroys the germs of the bladder.

2.8.6. Toothache

Make a paste of one teaspoon of cinnamon powder and five teaspoons of honey and apply on the aching tooth. This may be done 3 times a day daily till such time that the tooth has stopped aching.

2.8.7. Cholesterol

Two tablespoons of honey and three teaspoons of cinnamon powder mixed in 16 ounces of tea water if given to a cholesterol patient; it reduces the level of cholesterol in the body by 10 % within 2 hours. As mentioned for arthritic patients, if taken 3 times a day any chronic cholesterol cured. As per the information received in the said journal, pure honey taken with food daily relieves complains of cholesterol.

2.8.8. Colds

Those suffering from common or severe colds should take one tablespoon Luke warm honey with 1/4 teaspoon cinnamon powder daily for 3 days. This process will cure most chronic cough, cold and clear the sinuses.

2.8.9. Stomach upset

Honey taken with cinnamon powder cures stomachache and also clears stomach ulcers from the root. Gas: according to the studies done in India and Japan, it is revealed that if honey is taken with cinnamon powder the stomach is relieved of gas.

2.8.10. Heart Diseases

Make a paste of honey and cinnamon powder, apply on bread or chapatti instead of jelly and jam and eat it regularly for breakfast. It reduces the cholesterol in the arteries and saves the patient from heart attack. Also those who have already had an attack, if they do this process daily, are kept miles away from the next attack, regular use of the above process relieves loss of breath and strengthens the heart beat in America and Canada, various nursing homes have treated patients successfully and have found that due to the increasing age the arteries and veins, which lose their flexibility and get clogged, are revitalized.

2.8.11. Immune system

Daily use of honey and cinnamon powder strengthens the immune system and protects the body from bacterial and viral attacks. Scientists have found that honey has various vitamins and iron in large amounts. Constants use of honey strengthens the white blood corpuscles to fight bacterial and viral diseases.

2.8.12. Indigestion

Cinnamon powder sprinkled on two tablespoons of honey taken before food, relieves acidity and digests the heaviest of meals.

2.8.13. Influenza

A scientist in Spain has proved that honey contains a natural ingredient, which kills the influenza germs and saves the patient from flu.

2.8.14. Longevity

Tea made with honey and cinnamon powder, when taken regularly arrests the ravages of old age. Take 4 spoons of honey 1 spoon of cinnamon powder and 3 cups of water and boil to make like tea. Drink 1/4 cup, 3 to 4 times a day. It keeps the skin fresh and soft and arrests old age. Life spans also increases and even if a person is 100 years old. Starts performing the chores of 20 years old.

2.8.15. Pimples

Three tablespoons of honey and one teaspoon of cinnamon powder paste. Apply this paste on the pimples before sleeping and wash it next morning with warm water. If done daily for two weeks. It removes pimples from the roots.

2.8.16. Skin infections

Applying honey and cinnamon powder in equal parts on the affected parts cures eczema, ringworm and all types of skin infections.

2.8.17. Weight loss

Daily in the morning 1/2 hour before breakfast on an empty stomach and at night before sleeping, drink honey and cinnamon powder boiled in one cup water. If taken regularly it reduces the weight of even the most obese person. Also drinking of this mixture regularly does not allow the fat to accumulate in the body even though the person may eat a high calorie diet.

2.8.18. Cancer

Recent research in Japan and Australia has revealed that advanced cancer of the stomach and bones have been cured successfully. Patients suffering from these kinds of cancer should daily take one tablespoon of honey with one teaspoon of cinnamon powder for one month 3 times a day.

2.8.19. Fatigue

Recent studies have shown that the sugar content of honey is more helpful than detrimental to the body strength. Senior citizens who take honey and cinnamon powder in equal parts are more alert and flexible. Dr. Milton who has done research says that half tablespoon honey taken in one glass of water and sprinkled with cinnamon powder, taken daily after brushing and in the afternoon at about 3:00 p.m. When the vitality of the body starts decreasing. Increases the vitality of the body within a week.

2.8.20. Bad breath

People of South America, first thing in the morning gargle with one teaspoon of honey and cinnamon powder mixed in hot water. So, their breath stays fresh throughout the day.

2.8.21. Hearing loss

Daily morning and night honey and cinnamon powder taken in equal parts restores hearing.

2.8.22. Wound Healing

Honey is one of the oldest known medicines that have continued to be used up to present times in folk-medicine. Its use has been "rediscovered" in later times by the medical profession, especially for dressing wounds. The numerous reports of the effectiveness of honey in wound management, including reports of several randomised controlled trials, have recently been reviewed, rapid clearance of infection from the treated wounds being a commonly recorded observation.

In almost all of these reports honey is referred to generically, there being no indication given of any awareness of the variability that generally is found in natural products. Yet the ancient physicians were aware of differences in the therapeutic value of the honeys available to them: Aristotle (384-322 BC), discussing differences in honeys, referred to pale honey being "good as a salve for sore eyes and wounds"; and Dioscorides (50 AD) stated that a pale yellow honey from Attica was the best, being "good for all rotten and hollow ulcers". Any honey can be expected to suppress infection in wounds because of its high sugar content, but dressings of sugar on a wound have to be changed more frequently than honey dressings do to maintain an osmolarity that is inhibitory to bacteria, as honey has additional antibacterial components.

Since microbiological studies have shown more than one hundred-fold differences in the potency of the antibacterial activity of various honey, best results would be expected if a honey with a high level of antibacterial activity were used in the management of infected wounds. Other therapeutic properties of honey besides its antibacterial activity are also likely to vary. An anti-inflammatory action and a stimulatory effect on angiogenesis and on the growth of granulation tissue and epithelial cells have been observed clinically and in histological studies. The components responsible for these effects have not been identified, but the anti-inflammatory action may be due to antioxidants, the level of which varies in honey. The stimulation of tissue growth may be a trophic effect, as nutrification of wounds is known to hasten the healing process: the level of the wide range of micronutrients that occur in honey also varies. Until research is carried out to ascertain the components of honey responsible for all of its therapeutic effects it will not be possible to fully standardize honey to obtain optimal effectiveness in wound management. However, where an antiseptic wound dressing is required then standardization for this effect is possible.

Several brands of honey with standardized levels of antibacterial activity are commercially available in Australia and New Zealand, but even where these are not available it is possible to assay the level of antibacterial activity of locally available honey by a simple procedure in a microbiology laboratory.

3. MATERIALS AND METHODS

3.1. GENERAL METHODS

3.1.1. Cleaning of Glassware

All the glasswares were first soaked in cleaning solution (100 g of potassium dichromate was added to 100 ml of distilled water followed by addition of 50 ml of concentrated sulphuric acid for about 12 hours and washed in tap water. Then, they were boiled soap water and washed in tap water. Finally, they were cleaned in distilled water, dried and used for the study.

3.1.2. Sterilization

All the media were sterilized in autoclaves at 15 lbs/in^2 pressure for 15 minutes. The glasswares were sterilized at 160^{0}C for 1 hours in hot air oven.

3.1.3. Chemicals

The chemicals, organic solvents and reagents used in the study were of analytical reagent (AR) quality and the media were obtained from Hi-media Ltd., Mumbai.

3.2. HONEY SAMPLES SELECTED FOR PRESENT RESEARCH

a) Kombu Honey
b) Malan Honey
c) Commercial Honey

3.3. COLLECTION OF HONEY SAMPLES

The Natural and Commercial honey samples selected for the present study was collected from Chetheri Malai, Harur, Tamil Nadu, India.

3.4. COLLECTION OF TEST BACTERIAL CULTURES

Ten different bacterial cultures of were procured from Microbial Type Culture Collection (MTCC), India. The collected bacterial cultures are *Staphylococcus aureus, Bacillus cereus, Escherichia coli, Klebsiella pneumoniae, Shigella flexneri, Salmonella typhi, Acetobacter baumani, Proteus mirabilis, Micrococcus luteus* and *Pseudomonas aeruginosa*

3.5. CULTURE MAINTENANCE AND INOCULUM PREPARATION

3.5.1. Maintenance of bacterial cultures

The bacterial cultures were sub-cultured and maintained on Nutrient agar slants and stored in refrigerator at 4 °C.

3.5.2. Bacterial inoculum preparation

Bacterial inoculum was prepared by inoculating a loopful of bacteria in 5 ml of Nutrient broth and incubated at 37 °C for 12 hours till a moderate turbidity was developed. The turbidity was matched with 0.5 Mc Farland standard and then used for the determination of antibacterial activity.

3.6. DETERMINATION ANTIBACTERIAL ACTIVITY OF ESSENTIAL OILS

Mueller Hinton Agar plates were prepared and inoculated with test bacterial isolates by spreading the bacterial inoculum on the surface of the media. Wells (6 mm in diameter) were punched in the Mueller Hinton Agar. Honey samples with 75 µl/ml concentrations was mixed with 1 ml of Dimethyl sulfoxide (DMSO), mixed well and added into the well. Well containing DMSO alone act as a Negative control. The plates were incubated at 37 °C for 24 hours. The antibacterial activity was assessed by measuring the diameter of the zone of inhibition (in mm).

4. RESULTS AND DISCUSSION

Nowadays, honey is considered as a "Sweet Medicine" and it does not have any medicine hatters. Honey is the product with tremendous antimicrobial activity due to the presence of phenolic compounds and it is administered orally or topically. In older days, the honey was dipped in the dressing materials and used for dressing the various types of wounds. From older days to present days, the honey was mixed with coconut oil and used for treating peptic ulcer which was caused by *Helicobacter pylori*. In human diet, honey is playing a dual role. Honey in combination with the water was used for reducing the weight and in contrast honey in combination with milk was helped to increase the weight. Initially at the time of birth, a drop of honey was given to the infants to give the sweetness and nutrients. Various researchers reported the microcidal and microstatic activities of honey samples against pathogenic bacteria and fungi. The free radical scavenging activity of honey was studied and it finds a special place as Antioxidant agent too. Honey was also used as a preservative for the preservations of various food products which are easily prone to microbial spoilage (Kalidasan *et al.*, 2017). The present study was aimed to study the comparative analysis of Antibacterial activity, Anticandidal activity and Antioxidant activity of the two Natural honey (Kombu honey and Vembu honey) and two Commercially marketed honey.

The antimicrobial activity of three different Honey samples *viz.*, Kombu Honey, Malan Honey and Commercial Honey were evaluated against pathogenic bacteria (*Staphylococcus aureus, Micrococcus luteus, Bacillus cereus, Escherichia coli, Klebsiella pneumoniae, Salmonella typhi, Shigella flexneri, Proteus mirabilis, Pseudomonas aeruginosa* and *Acetobacter baumani*). The results of the present findings were given below.

4.1. ANTIBACTERIAL ACTIVITY OF KOMBU HONEY AGAINST BACTERIAL PATHOGENS

The antibacterial activity of Kombu honey was investigated against bacterial pathogens and the results were given in the Table - 1. Antibacterial activity was observed for all the ten bacterial isolates at 75 µl concentration. The Kombu honey showed maximum zone of inhibition against *Staphylococcus aureus* (34 mm) followed by *Micrococcus luteus* (32 mm), *Bacillus cereus* (30 mm), *Escherichia coli* (28 mm), *Klebsiella pneumoniae* (26 mm), *Salmonella typhi* (24 mm), *Proteus mirabilis* (24 mm) and *Pseudomonas aeruginosa* (23 mm). Minimum zone of inhibition was noticed in the pathogen *Acetobacter baumani* (22 mm). No zone of inhibition was seen in DMSO blind control.

Research has been conducted on manuka (*L. scoparium*) honey (Visavadia *et al.,* 2006), which has been demonstrated to be effective against several human pathogens, including *Escherichia coli, Enterobacter aerogenes, Salmonella typhimurium, Staphylococcus aureus* (Lusby *et al.,* 2005; Visavadia *et al.,* 2006). Many laboratory studies have revealed that the honey is effective against Methicillin-resistant *Staphylococcus aureus* (MRSA), β- haemolytic *Streptococci* and vancomycin resistant *Enterococci* (VRE) (Allen *et al.,* 2000 96; Kingsley, 2001 97). However, the newly identified honeys may have advantages over or similarities with manuka honey due to enhanced antimicrobial activity, local production (thus availability) and greater selectivity against medically important organisms (Lusby *et al.,* 2005). The coagulase negative *Staphylococci* are very similar to *Staphylococcus aureus* (Cooper *et al.,* 2002; Abhishek *et al.,* 2010) in their susceptibility to honey of similar antibacterial potency and more susceptible than *Pseudomonas aeruginosa* and *Enterococcus* species (Cooper *et al.,* 2002).

Gram positive bacteria such as *Staphylococcus aureus,* the causal agent of a range of illnesses from skin infections to life-threatening diseases such as pneumonia and meningitis, did not grow in the presence of honeys produced by *A. mellifera* and *Tetragonisca angustula* bees in the Brazilian states of Paraná and Minas Gerais. In order to study this effect, honeys were analysed by high performance liquid chormatography (HPLC) and the antimicrobial activity was connected to phenolic compounds, such as 4- hydroxybenzoic acid (HBEN). These compounds occur in higher concentrations in propolis than in honey and propolis was more effective against *Staphylococcus aureus* than honey (Miorin *et al.,* 2003). This bacterium has proved to be variable in susceptibility to different honeys. Turkish honeys from Anatolia showed a moderate inhibition towards some strains of *Staphylococcus aureus* (Kucuk *et al.,* 2007), while Turkish rhododendron honeys partially inhibited the growth of this bacterium (Silici *et al.,* 2010).

Honey from stingless bees had powerful activity against *Staphylococcus aureus* when compared to that exhibited by manuka honey produced by honeybees belonging to Apidae family (*A. mellifera, A. cerana*) (Temaru *et al.*, 2007). Argentinean honeys from the province of Cordoba evidenced high activity against *Staphylococcus aureus,* which was considered to be of remarkable clinical importance, since an increase in difficult-to-treat skin infections had been reported in the last decade and resistance against several antibiotics had developed (Basualdo *et al.*, 2007). A study of the properties of several Cuban honeys demonstrated that Gram positive bacteria are more sensitive than Gram negative bacteria with *Staphylococcus aureus* the most sensitive bacterium (Alvarez Suarez *et al.*, 2010).

Table – 1: Antibacterial activity of Kombu honey against bacterial pathogens

S.No	Bacterial pathogens	Kombu Honey at 75 µl/ml	DMSO
		Zone of inhibition (mm in dm)	**Zone of inhibition (mm in dm)**
1	*Staphylococcus aureus*	34	NZ
2	*Micrococcus luteus*	30	NZ
3	*Bacillus cereus*	32	NZ
4	*Escherichia coli*	28	NZ
5	*Salmonella typhi*	24	NZ
6	*Shigella flexneri*	25	NZ
7	*Klebsiella pneumoniae*	26	NZ
8	*Proteus mirabilis*	24	NZ
9	*Pseudomonas fluorescens*	23	NZ
10	*Acetobacter baumani*	22	NZ

NZ – No zone of inhibition

4.2. ANTIBACTERIAL ACTIVITY OF MALAN HONEY AGAINST BACTERIAL PATHOGENS

The antibacterial activity of Malan honey was studied against bacterial pathogens and the results were showed in the Table - 2. Antibacterial activity was noticed for all the ten bacterial isolates at 75 µl concentration. The Malan honey showed maximum zone of inhibition against *Staphylococcus aureus* (26 mm) followed by *Micrococcus luteus* (24 mm), *Bacillus cereus* (23 mm), *Shigella flexneri* (22 mm), *Pseudomonas aeruginosa* (21 mm), *Salmonella typhi* (21 mm), *Proteus mirabilis* (20 mm) and *Escherichia coli* (19 mm). Minimum zone of inhibition was noticed in *Acetobacter baumani* (17 mm). No zone of inhibition was seen in DMSO blind control. Baltrusaityte *et al.* (2007) observed that Lithuanian honeys exhibited antibacterial effects on *Staphylococcus aureus* and concluded that this was mainly due to the presence of hydrogen peroxide. Honeys produced in the Czech Republic are also antimicrobially effective with some honeydew honeys possessing the greatest effects (Vorlova *et al.*, 2005). In a study with unifloral and multifloral Portuguese honeys, Henriques *et al.* (2005) analyzed their antibacterial activity against a strain of *Staphylococcus aureus*, and observed that all of the samples tested possessed peroxide activity except some honeys derived from *Lavandula stoechas* which revealed non - peroxide antibacterial activity. Basson and Grobler (2008) found poor antibiotic activity of South African honeys from indigenous *L. cordifolium* and *Erica* species. Brudzynski and Miotto (2011) investigation with twenty Canadian unheated honeys, quantified Maillard reaction - like products (MRLPs) and total phenol contents, apart from assessing the antioxidant activity using the ORAC method. One of their results indicated that both the recorded antioxidant activity and the content of MRLPs of these honeys mainly contributed to the antibacterial activity against *Escherichia coli*. This antibacterial activity confirms the work of Rufian Henares and De La Cueva (2009) who suggested that the antibacterial activity of coffee melanoidins against *Escherichia coli* is due to their behavior as metalchelators.

Table – 2: Antibacterial activity of Malan Honey against bacterial pathogens

S. No	Bacterial pathogens	Malan Honey at 75 µl/ml	DMSO
		Zone of inhibition (mm in dm)	Zone of inhibition (mm in dm)
1	*Staphylococcus aureus*	26	NZ
2	*Micrococcus luteus*	23	NZ
3	*Bacillus cereus*	24	NZ
4	*Escherichia coli*	19	NZ
5	*Salmonella typhi*	21	NZ
6	*Shigella flexneri*	22	NZ
7	*Klebsiella pneumoniae*	18	NZ
8	*Proteus mirabilis*	20	NZ
9	*Pseudomonas fluorescens*	21	NZ
10	*Acetobacter baumani*	17	NZ

NZ – No zone of inhibition

4.3. ANTIBACTERIAL ACTIVITY OF COMMERCIAL HONEY AGAINST BACTERIAL PATHOGENS

The antibacterial activity of Commercial honey was tested against bacterial pathogens and the results were tabulated in the Table - 3. Antibacterial activity was recorded for all the ten bacterial isolates at 75 µl concentration. The Commercial honey showed maximum zone of inhibition against *Staphylococcus aureus* (22 mm) followed by *Micrococcus luteus* (21 mm), *Bacillus cereus* (20 mm), *Salmonella typhi* (19 mm), *Shigella flexneri* (19 mm), *Pseudomonas aeruginosa* (18 mm), *Escherichia coli* (17 mm), *Acetobacter baumani* (17 mm) and *Klebsiella pneumoniae* (16 mm). Minimum zone of inhibition was noticed in *Proteus mirabilis* (15 mm). No zone of inhibition was seen in DMSO blind control.

Isla *et al.* (2011) observed that algarrobo honey (*Prosopis nigra*) and a multifloral honey from the northwestern provinces of Argentina had activity against *Staphylococcus aureus.* They identified at least five antibacterial compounds in the algarrobo honey and four compounds in the multifloral honey and found that most of them corresponded to flavonoids. One of these flavonoids was identified as pinocembrin. The authors also pointed out that the antibacterial activity of the analysed honeys might be mainly due to their phenol content because of the significant correlation observed between the phenolic content and the antibacterial activity.

Some other honey sensitive - pathogens described in the literature are *Bacillus anthrasis* (anthrax), *Corynebacterium diptheriae* (diphtheria), *Klebsiella pneumoniae* (pneumonia), *Mycobacterium tuberculosis* (tuberculosis), *Salmonella typhi* (typhoid fever), *Vibrio cholerae* (cholera) and different *Streptococci,* among others. For example, *Klebsiella pneumoniae* was found to be sensitive to Argentinean (Basualdo *et al.*, 2007), and Thai honeys (Srisayam and Chantawannakul, 2010). The growth of *Enterococcus faecalis* was inhibited by stingless honeybee honey (Temaru *et al.*, 2007) and this bacterium also showed sensitivity to honey according to the research performed by Gallardo - Chacon *et al.* (2008).

In addition, other bacteria sensitive to different types of honey are *Staphylococcus epidermidis* (Basualdo *et al.*, 2007; Baltrusaityte, 2007), *Staphylococcus uberis* (Basualdo *et al.*, 2007), *Pediococcus mirabilis* (Silici *et al.*, 2010), *Aeromonas hydrophila* (Silici *et al.*, 2010), *Micrococcus luteus* (Srisayam and Chantawannakul, 2010), *Streptococcus oralis* (Basson and Grobler, 2008), *Streptococcus anginosus* (Basson and Grobler, 2008), *Salmonella enterica* ser. *typhimurium* (Vorlova *et al.*, 2005; Gallardo Chacón *et al.*, 2008), *Shigella sonnei* (Gallardo Chacon *et al.*, 2008), *Listeria monocytogenes* (Vorlova *et al.*, 2005; Gallardo Chacon *et al.*, 2008) and *Streptococcus mutans* (Basson and Grobler, 2008). Among yeasts, some *Candida* species were inhibited by Turkish honeys (Kucuk *et al.*, 2007).

The initial event in the development of bacterial infections of the gastrointestinal gut is the attachment of bacteria to the mucosal epithelial cells (Raupach *et al.*, 1999) and the blocking of this event represents an interesting strategy for the prevention of diseases (O´Farrelly *et al.*, 1992; Peralta *et al.*, 1994). Alnaqdy *et al.* (2005) studied the antimicrobial activity of Omani honeys against *Salmonella interitidis* and the ability of these honeys to prevent the bacterium from adhering to intestinal epithelial cells *in vitro*. Among the Gram negative bacteria, *Escherichia coli* is of great concern from a health point of view. It may cause life threatening gastric infections and diarrhoea, following consumption of contaminated food, as well as other infections such as cystitis, meningitis, peritonitis and pneumonia. There are several studies on the antibiotic effect of honey towards *Escherichia coli.* The *Escherichia coli* exhibited sensitivity to stingless honeybee honey (Temaru *et al.*, 2007), Spanish honeys (Gallardo - Chacon *et al.*, 2008), Cuban honeys (Alvarez - Suarez *et al.*, 2010), and Thailand honeys (Srisayam and Chantawanakul, 2010).

Table – 3: Antibacterial activity of Commercial honey against bacterial pathogens

S. No	Bacterial pathogens	Commercial Honey at 75 µl/ml	DMSO
		Zone of inhibition (mm in dm)	Zone of inhibition (mm in dm)
1	*Staphylococcus aureus*	22	NZ
2	*Micrococcus luteus*	20	NZ
3	*Bacillus cereus*	21	NZ
4	*Escherichia coli*	17	NZ
5	*Salmonella typhi*	19	NZ
6	*Shigella flexneri*	19	NZ
7	*Klebsiella pneumoniae*	16	NZ
8	*Proteus mirabilis*	15	NZ
9	*Pseudomonas fluorescens*	18	NZ
10	*Acetobacter baumani*	17	NZ

NZ – No zone of inhibition

ANTIBACTERIAL ACTIVITY OF HONEY SAMPLES AGAINST BACTERIAL PATHOGENS

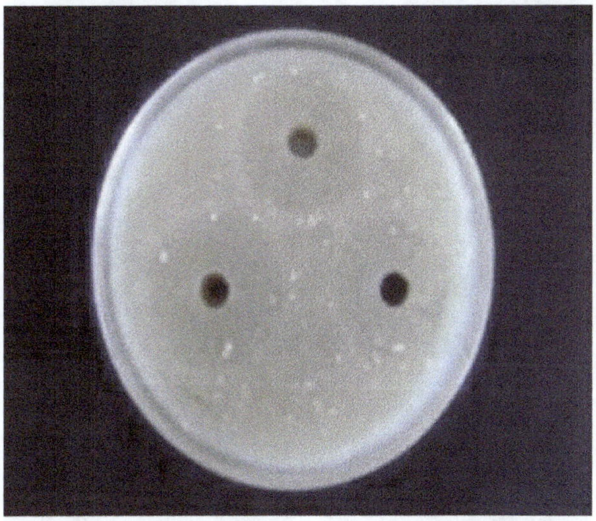

Staphylococcus aureus

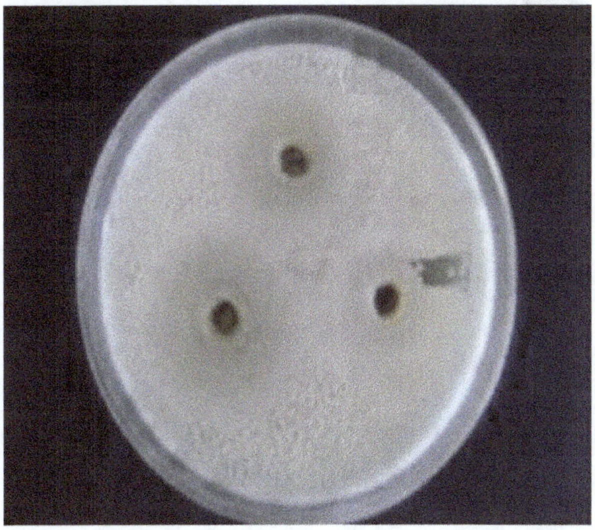

Salmonella typhi

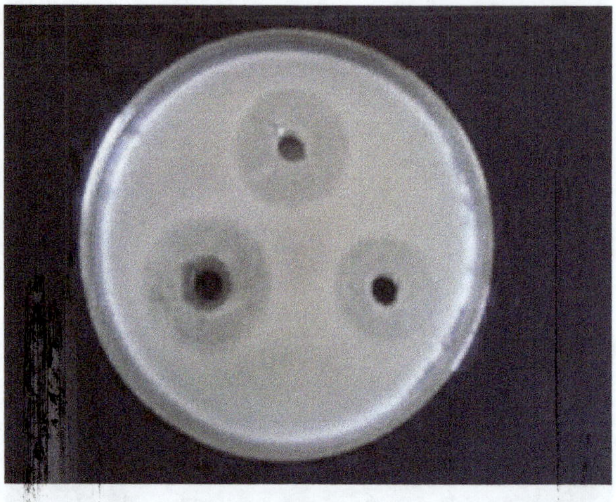

Escherichia coli

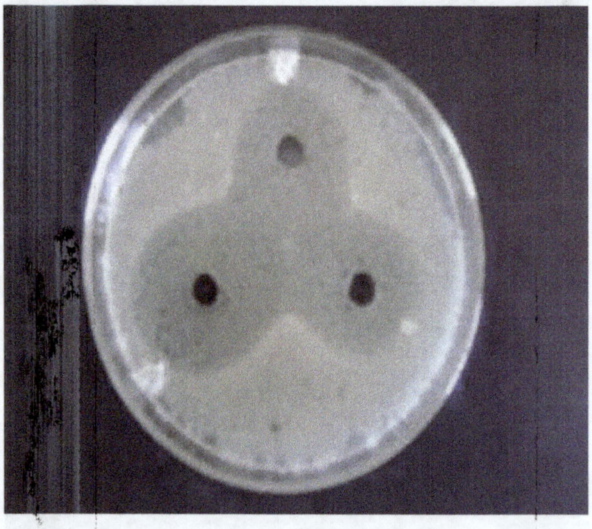

Klebsiella pneumoniae

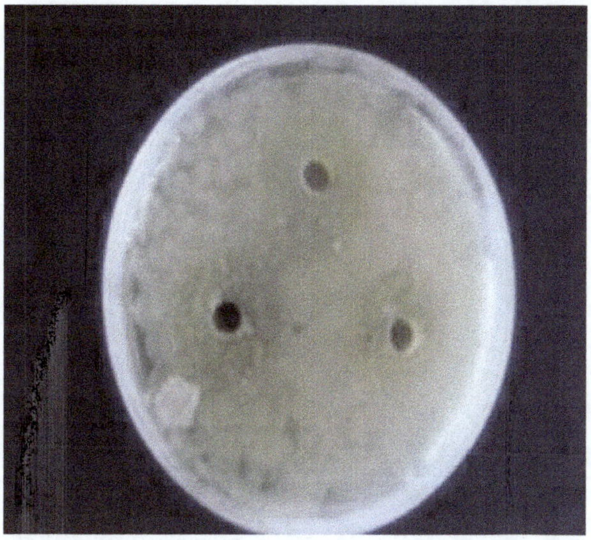

Micrococcus luteus

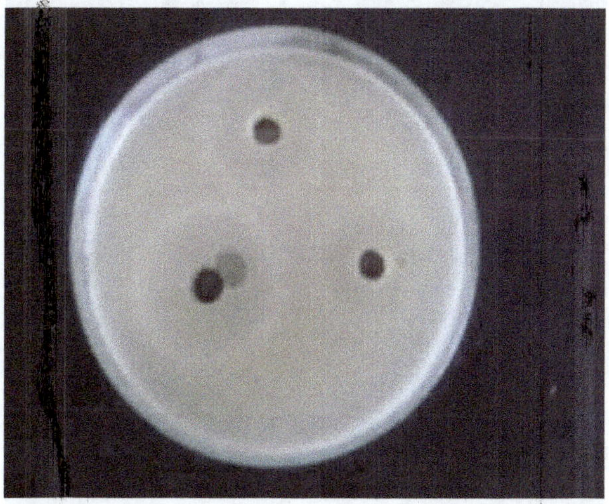

Bacillus cereus

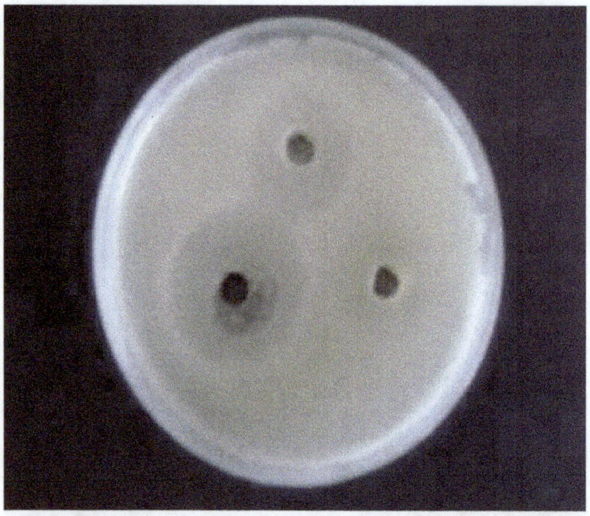

Proteus mirabilis

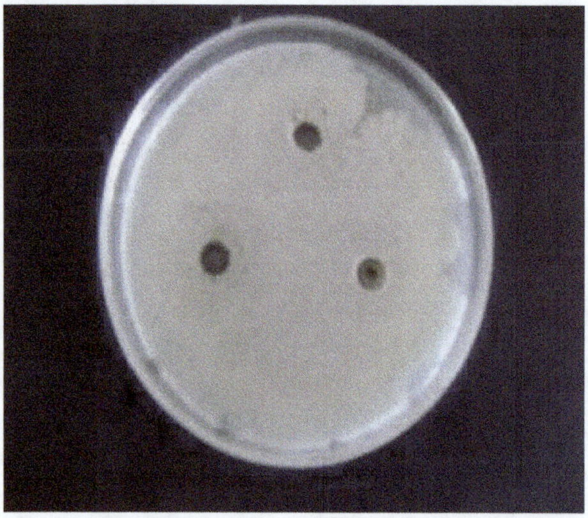

Shigella flexneri

4. SUMMARY

- The antimicrobial activity of three different Honey samples *viz.*, Kombu Honey, Malan Honey and Commercial Honey were evaluated against pathogenic bacteria (*Staphylococcus aureus, Micrococcus luteus, Bacillus cereus, Escherichia coli, Klebsiella pneumoniae, Salmonella typhi, Shigella flexneri, Proteus mirabilis, Pseudomonas aeruginosa* and *Acetobacter baumani*).
- The Natural and Commercial honey samples selected for the present study was collected from Chetheri Malai, Harur, Tamil Nadu, India.
- The antibacterial activity of Kombu honey was investigated against bacterial pathogens. The Kombu honey showed maximum zone of inhibition against *Staphylococcus aureus* (34 mm) followed by *Micrococcus luteus* (32 mm), *Bacillus cereus* (30 mm), *Escherichia coli* (28 mm), *Klebsiella pneumoniae* (26 mm), *Salmonella typhi* (24 mm), *Proteus mirabilis* (24 mm) and *Pseudomonas aeruginosa* (23 mm). Minimum zone of inhibition was noticed in the pathogen *Acetobacter baumani* (22 mm).
- The antibacterial activity of Malan honey was studied against bacterial pathogens. The Malan honey showed maximum zone of inhibition against *Staphylococcus aureus* (26 mm) followed by *Micrococcus luteus* (24 mm), *Bacillus cereus* (23 mm), *Shigella flexneri* (22 mm), *Pseudomonas aeruginosa* (21 mm), *Salmonella typhi* (21 mm), *Proteus mirabilis* (20 mm) and *Escherichia coli* (19 mm). Minimum zone of inhibition was noticed in *Acetobacter baumani* (17 mm).

- The antibacterial activity of Commercial honey was tested against bacterial pathogens. The Commercial honey showed maximum zone of inhibition against *Staphylococcus aureus* (22 mm) followed by *Micrococcus luteus* (21 mm), *Bacillus cereus* (20 mm), *Salmonella typhi* (19 mm), *Shigella flexneri* (19 mm), *Pseudomonas aeruginosa* (18 mm), *Escherichia coli* (17 mm), *Acetobacter baumani* (17 mm) and *Klebsiella pneumoniae* (16 mm). Minimum zone of inhibition was noticed in *Proteus mirabilis* (15 mm).
- Kombu honey exhibited more antimicrobial activity against bacterial pathogens when compared to the Malan honey and Commercial honey.

5. CONCLUSION

The present research concluded that the Kombu honey exhibited more antimicrobial activity against bacterial pathogens when compared to the Malan honey and Commercial honey. Comparatively, the activity of Commercial honey was very less when compared to the Natural honey samples. Further, since honey is a cheap, easily available and also a non-toxic antimicrobial agent due to its properties, it can be very effectively used for medical purposes. On the basis of present study, it is suggested that further broad spectrum studies as well as clinical trials should be conducted before the use of these products as routine medicines. New studies based on a chemical, pharmacological, and clinical approach must be conducted.

6. REFERENCES

1) Abhishek, K. J., Ravichandran, V., Madhvi, S. and Agrawal, R. K. 2010. Synthesis and antibacterial evaluation of substituted 4, 5- diphenyl-N-alkyl imidazole derivatives. *Asian Pacific Journal of Tropical Medicine*, 3 (6): 472 - 474.
2) Adams, C. J., Boult, C. H., Deadman, B. J., Farr, J. M., Grainger, M.N.C and Manley-Harris, M. 2008. Isolation by HPLC and characterization of the bioactive fraction of New Zealand manuka (*Leptospermum scoparium*) honey. *Carbohydrate Research*, 343: 651-659.
3) Adams, C. J., Manley Harris, M and Molan, P. C. 2009. The origin of methylglyoxal in New Zealand manuka (*Leptospermum scoparium*) honey. *Carbohydrate Research,* 344: 1050 - 1053.
4) Adeleke, O. E., Olaitan, J. O. and Okepekpe, E. I. 2006. Comparative antibacterial activity of honey and gentamicin against *Escherichia coli* and *Pseudomonas aeruginosa. Annals Burn Fire Disasters*, 19: 4.
5) Ahmed, A. K., Hoekstra, M. J., Hage, J. and Karim, R. B. 2003. Honey-medicated dressing: transformation of an ancient remedy into modern therapy. *Annals of Plastic Surgery*, 50: 143 - 148.
6) Al Waili, N. S. 2004. Topical honey application vs acyclovir for the treatment of recurrent herpes simplex lesions. *Medical Science Monitoring*, 10 (8): 94 - 98.
7) Allen, K. L., Hutchinson, G. and Molan, P. C. 2000. The potential for using honey to treat wounds infected with MRSA and VRE. First World Healing Congress, Melbourne, Australia; 10 - 13.
8) Allen, K. L., Molan, P. C. and Reid, G. M. 1991. A survey of the antibacterial activity of some New Zealand honeys. *Journal of Pharmacy and Parmacology*, 43: 817 - 822.

9) Alnaqdy, A., Al-Jabri, A., Al Mahrooqi, Z., Nzeako, B. and Nsanze, H. 2005. Inhibition effect of honey on the adherence of *Salmonella* to intestinal epithelial cells *in vitro*. *International Journal of Food Microbiology*, 103: 347 - 351.

10) Alvarez Suarez, J. M., Tulipani, S., Diaz, S., Estevez, Y., Romandini, S., Giampieri, F., Damiani, E., Astolfi, P., Bompadre, S. and Battino, M. 2010. Antioxidant and antimicrobial capacity of several monofloral Cuban honeys and their correlation with color, polyphenol content and other chemical compounds. *Food and Chemical Toxicology*, 48: 2490 - 2499.

11) Alves Da Silva, R., Arraes Maia, G., Machado De Souza, P H. and Correia Da Costa, J. M. 2006. Composição e propriedades terapêuticas do mel de abelha. *Alimentos Nutrição,* 17 (1): 113 - 120.

12) Al-Waili, N. S. 2003. Topical application of natural honey, beeswax and olive oil mixture for atopic dermatitis or psoriasis: partially controlled, single - blinded study. *Complementary Therapies in Medicine*, 11(4): 226 – 234.

13) Al-Waili, N. S. 2004. Natural honey lowers plasma glucose, C-reactive protein, homocysteine, and blood lipids in healthy, diabetic, and hyperlipidemic subjects: Comparison with dextrose and sucrose. *Journal of Medicine and Food*, 7: 100 – 107.

14) Al-Waili, N. S., Akmal, M., Al-Waili, F. S., Saloom, K. Y. and Ali, A. 2005. The antimicrobial potential of honey from United Arab Emirates on some microbial isolates. *Medical Science Monitor*, 11: 433 - 438.

15) Amabile - Cuevas, C. F. 2006. Antimicrobial resistance in bacteria. Horzon Bioscience, Mexico.

16) Anklam, E. 1998. A review of the analytical methods to determine the geographical and botanical origin of honey. *Food Chemistry*, 63 (4): 549 - 562.

17) Armstrong, S. and Otis, G. W. 1995. The antibacterial properties of honey. *Bee Culture,* 123 (9): 500 - 502.

18) Aronne, G and Micco, D. E. 2010. Traditional melissopalynology integrated by multivariate analysis and sampling methods to improve botanical and geographical characterization of honeys. *Plant Biosynthesis,* 144: 833 - 840.

19) Assia, A and Ali, L. 2015. Enzymes activities, hydroxymethylfurfural content and pollen spectrum of some Algerian honey. *African Journal of Agricultural Research,* 10: 613 - 622.

20) Attrot, J. and Henle, T. 2009. Methylglyoxal in Manuka honey - Correlation with antibacterial properties. *Czech Journal of Food Science*, 27: S163 - S165.

21) Aysan, E., Ayar, E., Aren, A and Cifter, C. 2002. The role of intraperitoneal honey administration in preventing postoperative peritoneal adhesions. *European Journal of Gynecology and Reproduction Biology,* 104(2): 152 – 155.

22) Babacan, S., Pivarnik, L. F. and Rand, A. G. 2002. Honey amylase activity and food starch degradation. *Journal of Food Science*, 67 (5): 1625 - 1630.

23) Badawy, O.F.H., Shafii, S.S.A., Tharwat, E.E. and Kamal, A. M. 2004. Antibacterial activity of bee honey and its therapeutic usefulness against *Escherichia coli* O157:H7 and *Salmonella typhimurium* infection. *Reviews in Science and Technology*, 23: 1011 - 1122.

24) Baltrusaityte, V., Venskutonis, P. R. and Ceksteryte, V. 2007. Antibacterial activity of honey and beebread of different origin against *Staphylococcus aureus* and *Staphylococcus epidermis. Food Technology and Biotechnology*, 45 (2): 201 - 208.

25) Bang L. M., Buntting C and Molan P. 2003. Peroxide production in honey and its implications. *Journal of Alternative and Complement Medicine*, 9: 267 - 273.

26) Baroni, M. V., Nores, M. L., Diaz Mdel, P., Chiabrando, G. A., Fassano, J. P., Costa, C and Wunderlin, D. A. 2006. Determination of volatile organic compound patterns characteristic of five unifloral honey by solid-phase

microextraction-gas chromatography-mass spectrometry coupled to chemometrics. *Journal of Agricultural and Food Chemistry,* 54: 7235 - 7241.

27) Basson, N. J. and Grobler, S. R. 2008. Antimicrobial activity of two South African honeys produced from indigenous *Leucospermum cordifolium* and *Erica* species on selected microorganisms. *BMC Complementary and Alternative Medicine*, 15 (8): 41.

28) Basualdo, C., Sgroy, V., Finola, M. S. and Juam, M. 2007. Comparison of the antibacterial activity of honey from different provenance against bacteria usually isolated from skin wounds. *Veterinary Microbiology*, 124: 375 - 381.

29) Bauer, A. W., Kirby, W. M. M., Sherris, J. C and Turck, M. 1966. Antibiotic susceptibility testing by a standardized single disk method. *American Journal of Clinical Pathology*, 45 (4): 493 - 496.

30) Beck, B. F and Smedley D. 1997. Honey and your health. New York, McBride Publishing (originally published in 1944).

31) Berenbaum, M., Robinson, G. and Unnevehr, L. 1996. Antioxidant properties of Illinois honeys. Grant Proposal for National Honey Board. University of Illinois at Urbana - Champaign.

32) Bertrams, J., Kunz, N., Müller, M., Kammerer, D and Stintzing, F. C. 2013. Phenolic compounds as marker compounds for botanical origin determination of German propolis samples based on TLC and TLC-MS. *Journal of Applied Botany and Food Quality,* 86: 143 – 153.

33) Beutler, J. A. 2009. Natural products as a foundation for drug discovery. *Current Protocols in Pharmacology*, 46: 115 - 122.

34) Bharathi, T., Kolanjinathan, K. and Saranraj, P. 2014. Antimicrobial activity of solvent extracts of *Ocimum sanctum*, *Azadirachta indica* and *Phyllanthus amarus* against clinical pathogens. *Global Journal of Pharmacology*, 8 (3): 294 – 305.

35) Blair, S. E., Cokcetin, N. N., Harry, E. J and Carter, D. A. 2009. The unusual antibacterial activity of medical-grade *Leptospermum* honey: antibacterial spectrum, resistance and transcriptome analysis. *European Journal of Clinical Microbiology and Infectious Diseases,* 28: 1199 – 1208.

36) Blassa, M., Candracci, M., Accorsi, A., Piacentini, M. P., Albertini, M. C., Piatti, E. 2006. Raw millefiori honey is packed full of antioxidants. *Food Chemistry*, 97: 217 - 222.

37) Bobis, O., Marghitas, L., Rindt, I. K., Niculae, M and Dezmirean, D. 2008. Honeydew honey: correlations between Chemical composition, antioxidant capacity and Antibacterial effect. *Lucrări stiinŃifice Zootehnie si Biotehnologii,* 41(2): 271- 2 77.

38) Bogdanov, S. 1989. Determination of pinocembrin in honey using HPLC. *Journal of Apicultural Research*, 28 (1): 55 - 57.

39) Bogdanov, S. 2006. Contaminants of bee products. *Apidologie*, 38: 1 - 18.

40) Bogdanov, S., Martin P and Lüllman, C. 1997. Harmonised methods of the European Honey Comission. *Apidologie,* 3: 1 - 59.

41) Bogdanov, S., Ruoff, K and Oddo, L. P. 2004. Physico-chemical methods for the characterization of unifloral honeys: a review. *Apidologie*, 35: S4 - S17.

42) Boukraa, L. and Niar, A. 2007. Sahara honeys shows higher potency against *Pseudomonas aeruginosa* compared to north Algerian types of honey. *Journal of Medicinal Food*, 10 (4): 712 - 714.

43) Brady, N., Molan, P and Bang, L. 2004. A survey of non-manuka New Zealand honeys for antibacterial and antifungal activities. *Journal of Apiculture Research*, 43: 47 – 52.

44) Brudzynski, K and Kim, L. 2011. Storage induced chemical changes in active components of honey deregulate its antibacterial activity. *Food Chemistry*, 126: 1155 - 1163.

45) Brudzynski, K and Lannigan, R. 2012. Mechanism of honey bacteriostatic action against MRSA and VRE involves hydroxyl radicals generated from honey's hydrogen peroxide. *Frontiers in microbiology,* 3: 36 - 40.

46) Brudzynski, K. and Miotto, D. 2011. The relationship between the content of Maillard reaction - like products and bioactivity of Canadian honeys. *Food Chemistry*, 124: 869 – 874.

47) Brudzynski, K., Abubaker, K and Miotto, D. 2012. Unraveling a mechanism of honey antibacterial action: Polyphenol or H_2O_2 - induced oxidative effect on bacterial cell growth and on DNA degradation. *Food Chemistry,* 133: 329 - 336.

48) Brudzynski, K., Abubaker, K., Laurent, M and Castle, A. 2011. Re-examining the role of hydrogen peroxide in bacteriostatic and bactericidal activities of honey. *Frontiers in microbiology,* 2: 213.

49) Bruggink, A., Roos, E. C and De Vroom, E. 1998. Penicillin acylase in the industrial production of β-lactam antibiotics. *Organic Process Research and Development,* 2: 128 - 133.

50) Bruni, I., Galimberti, A., Caridi, L., Scaccabarozzi, D., De Mattia, F., Casiraghi, M and Labra, M. 2015. A DNA barcoding approach to identify plant species in multiflower honey. *Food Chemistry,* 170: 308 - 315.

51) Bucekova, M., Valachova, I., Kohutova, L., Prochazka, E., Klaudiny, J and Majtan, J. 2014. Honeybee glucose oxidase - its expression in honeybee workers and comparative analyses of its content and H_2O_2 - mediated antibacterial activity in natural honeys. *Nature* 101: 661 - 670.

52) Butler, M. S., Robertson, A. B and Cooper, M. A. 2014. Natural product and natural product derived drugs in clinical trials. *Natural Product Reports,* 31, 1612 - 1661.

53) Cai, Y., Luo, Q., Sun, M and Corke, H. 2004. Antioxidant activity and phenolic compounds of 112 traditional Chinese medicinal plants associated with anticancer. *Life Sciences,* 74: 2157 - 2184.

54) Casteels, P., Ampe, C., Jacobs, F and Tempst, P. 1993. Functional and chemical characterization of Hymenoptaecin, an antibacterial polypeptide that is infection-inducible in the honeybee (*Apis mellifera*). *Journal of Biological Chemistry,* 268: 7044 - 7054.

55) Castro-Vazquez, L., Diaz - Maroto, M. C., González - Viñas, M. A., De La Fuente, E and Pérez - Coello, M. S. 2008. Influence of storage conditions on chemical composition and sensory properties of citrus honey. *Journal of Agricultural and Food Chemistry,* 56: 1999 - 2006.

56) Chritchfield, J. W., Butera, S. T. and Folks, T. M. 1995. Inhibition of HIV-1 activation in chronically infected cells by flavonoid compounds. National Conference on Human Retroviruses and Related Infections, Washington DC, Retrovirus Diseases Branch, Centers for Disease Control and Prevention, Atlanta, GA.

57) Conti, M. E. 2000. Lazio region (Central Italy) honeys: a survey of mineral content and typical quality parameters. *Food Control,* 11: 459 – 463.

58) Cooper, R. A., Halas, E and Molan, P. C. 2002. The efficacy of honey in inhibiting strains of *Pseudomonas aeruginosa* from infected burns. *The Journal of Burn Care and Rehabilitation,* 23: 366 - 370.

59) Cooper, R. A., Molan, P. C. and Harding, K. G. 1999. Antibacterial activity of honey against strains of *Staphylococcus aureus* from infected wounds. *Journal of Research in Society and Medicine*, 92: 283 - 285.

60) Cortes, M. E., Vigil, P and Montenegro, G. 2011. The medicinal value of honey: a review on its benefits to human health, with a special focus on its effects on glycemic regulation. *Bioresource Technology,* 38(2): 303 - 317.

61) Cragg, G. M and Newman, D. J. 2013. Natural products: a continuing source of novel drug leads. *Biochimica et Biophysica Acta,* 1830: 3670 - 3695.

62) Crane, E and Visscher, P. K. 2009. Chapter 121 - Honey, In: Vincent H. Resh and Ring T. Carde, Editor(s), Encyclopedia of Insects (Second Edition), Academic Press, San Diego, Pages 459-461.

63) Crane, E. 1975. Honey - A comprehensive survey. First Heinemann London.

64) Crane, E. 1976. "Honey: A Comprehensive Survey," Corrected edition. International Bee Research Association/Heinemann, London.

65) Crane, E. 1999. The World History of Beekeeping and Honey Hunting. Gerald Duckworth and Co. Ltd, London.

66) Cuevas Glory, L. F., Pino, J. A., Santiago, L. S and Sauri-Duch, E. 2007. A review of volatile analytical methods for determining the botanical origin of honey. *Food Chemistry,* 103: 1032 - 1043.

67) Darwina, M., Kanchana, D and Saranraj, P. 2012. Biocontrol efficacy of various preservatives against food borne pathogens in poultry chicken. *Novus International Journal of Biotechnology and Biosciences*, 1 (1): 1 - 13

68) David, B., Wolfender, J. L and Dias, D. 2014. The pharmaceutical industry and natural products: historical status and new trends. *Phytochemistry Reviews*, 36: 1 - 17.

69) Davidson, B. S. 1995. New dimensions in natural products research: cultured marine microorganisms. *Current Opinion in Biotechnology,* 6: 284 - 291.

70) Derek, D., Schramm, D., Malina Karim, T., Heather R. Schrader, Roberta R. Holt, Marcia Cardetti and Carl L. Keen. 2013. *Journal of Agriculture and Food Chemistry*, 51(6): 1732 – 1735.

71) Deurenberg, R. H and Stobberingh, E. E. 2008. The evolution of Staphylococcus aureus. *Infection, Genetics and Evolution,* 8: 747 - 763.

72) Dixon, R. A and Pasinetti, G. M. 2010. Flavonoids and isoflavonoids: from plant biology to agriculture and neuroscience. *Plant Physiology,* 154: 453 - 457.

73) Dong, R., Zheng, Y and Xu, B. 2013. Phenolic profiles and antioxidant capacities of chinese unifloral honeys from different botanical and geographical sources. *Food and Bioprocess Technology,* 6: 762 - 770.

74) Dossey, A. T. 2010. Insects and their chemical weaponry: New potential for drug discovery. *Natural Product Reports,* 27: 1737 - 1757.

75) Du Toit, D. F. and Page, B. J. 2009. An *in vitro* evaluation of the cell toxicity of honey and silver dressings. *Journal of Wound Care*, 18 (9): 383 - 389.

76) Eldridge, G. R., Vervoort, H. C., Lee, C. M., Cremin, P. A., Williams, C. T., Hart, S. M., Goering, M. G., O'neil - Johnso, M and Zeng, L. 2002. High - Throughput Method for the Production and Analysis of Large Natural Product Libraries for Drug Discovery. *Analytical Chemistry,* 74: 3963 - 3971.

77) Ensminger, A. H., Ensminger, M. E., Konlande, J. E. and Robson, J. R. K. 1983. “Food and Nutrition Encyclopedia”. Pegus Press, Clovis, CA.

78) Erlanson, D. 2012. Introduction to fragment-based drug discovery. *In:* DAVIES, T. G. & HYVÖNEN, M. (eds.) *Fragment-Based Drug Discovery and X-Ray Crystallography.* Springer Berlin Heidelberg.

79) Escuredo, O., Silva, L. R., Valentão, P., Seijo, M. C and Andrade, P. B. 2012. Assessing *Rubus* honey value: Pollen and phenolic compounds content and antibacterial capacity. *Food Chemistry,* 130: 671 - 678.

80) Fangio, M. F., Iurlina, M. O. and Fritz, R. 2010. Characterization of Argentinean honeys and evaluation of its inhibitory action on *Escherichia coli* growth. *International Journal of Food Science and Technology*, 45: 520 - 529.

81) Fleming, A. 1929. On the antibacterial action of cultures of a *penicillium*, with special reference to their use in the isolation of *B. influenzae*. *International Journal of Experimental Pathology,* 10: 226 - 236.

82) Flodhazi, G. 1994. Analysis and quantification of sugars in honey of different botanical origin using high performance liquid chromatography. *Acta Alimentaria*, 23 (3): 299 -311.

83) Fontana, R., Mendes, M. A., Souza, B. M. D., Konno, K., Cesar, L. L. M. M., Malaspina, O and Palma, M. S. 2004. Jelleines: a family of antimicrobial peptides from the Royal Jelly of honeybees (*Apis mellifera*). *Peptides,* 25: 919 - 928.

84) Fournier, P. and Dupuis, Y. 1975. Modulation of intestinal absorption of calcium. *Journal of Physiology*, 70: 479 - 491.

85) Frankel, S. Robinson, G. E. and Berenbaum, M. R. 1998. Antioxidant capacity and correlated characteristics of unifloral honeys. *Journal of Apicultural Research*, 37 (1): 27-31.

86) Free, J. B. 1982. Bees and mankind. Boston: George Allen and Unwin.

87) French, V. M., Cooper, R. A. and Molan, P. C. 2005. The antibacterial activity of honey against Coagulase - negative *Staphylococci. Journal of Antimicrobial Chemotherapy*, 56: 228 - 231.

88) Galimberti, A., De Mattia, F., Bruni, I., Scaccabarozzi, D., Sandionigi, A., Barbuto, M., Casiraghi, M and Labra, M. 2014. A DNA barcoding approach to characterize pollen collected by honeybees. *PLoS ONE,* 9: e109363.

89) Gallardo Chacon, J. J., Caselles, M., Izquierdo Pulido, M. and Rius, N. 2008. Inhibitory activity of monofloral and multifloral honeys against bacterial pathogens. *Journal of Apicultural Research*, 47 (2): 131 - 136.

90) Ganesh, P., Sureshkumar, R. and Saranraj, P. 2014. Phytochemical analysis and antibacterial activity of Pepper (*Piper nigrum* L.) against some human pathogens. *Central European Journal of Experimental Biology*, 3 (2): 36 – 41.

91) Gheldof, N and Engeseth, N. J. 2002. Antioxidant capacity of honeys from various floral sources based on the determination of oxygen radical absorbance capacity and inhibition of in vitro lipoprotein oxidation in human serum samples. *Journal of Agriculture and Food Chemistry*, 50: 3050 – 3055.

92) Golob, T., Dobersek, U., Kump, P and Necemer, M. 2005. Determination of trace and minor elements in Slovenian honey by total reflection X-ray fluorescence spectroscopy. *Food Chemistry*, 91: 593 – 600.

93) Gomez - Caravaca, A. M., Gomez - Romero, M., Arraez – Roman, D., Segura Carretero, A. and Fernandez – Gutierrez, A. 2006. Advances in the analysis of phenolic compounds in products derived from bees. *Journal of Pharmaceutical and Biological Annals*, 41: 1220 -1234.

94) Haffejee, I. E and Moosa, A. 1985. Honey in the treatment of infantile gastroenteritis. *Brazil Medical Journal,* 290: 1866 - 1867.

95) Harvey, A. 2000. Strategies for discovering drugs from previously unexplored natural products. *Drug Discovery Today,* 5: 294 - 300.

96) Harvey, A. L., Edrada Ebel, R and Quinn, R. J. 2015. The re-emergence of natural products for drug discovery in the genomics era. *Nature Reviews Drug Discovery,* 14: 111 - 129.

97) Havenhand, G. 2010. London, UK, Kyle Cathie Limited.

98) Henriques, A. F. F. M. 2006. The antibacterial activity of honey. PhD Thesis. University of Wales Institute Cardiff.

99) Henriques, A. F., Jenkins, R. E., Burton, N.F and Cooper, R. A. 2010. The intracellular effects of manuka honey on *Staphylococcus aureus. European Journal of Clinical Microbiology and Infectious Disease*, 29(1): 45 - 50.

100) Henriques, A., Burton, N. F. and Cooper, R. A. 2005. Antibacterial activity of selected Portuguese honeys. *Journal of Apicultural Research*, 44 (3): 119 - 123.

101) Henriques, A., Jackson, S., Cooper, R. and Burton, N. 2006. Free radical production and quenching in honeys with wound healing potential. *Journal of Antimicrobial Chemotherapy*, 58: 773 - 777.

102) Hopkins, B. J., Hodgson, W. C and Sutherland, S. K. 1994. Pharmacological studies of stonefish (*Synanceja trachynis*) venom. *Toxicon,* 32: 1197 - 1210.

103) Hu, Ch-Q; Chen, K; Shi, Q; Kilkuskie, R E; Cheng, Y C; Lee, K H 1994. Anti-AIDS agents, 10. Acacetin – 7 – O – β – D - galactopyranoside, an anti-HIV principle from *Chrysanthemum morifolium* and a structure-activity correlation with some related flavonoids. *Journal of Natural Products*, 57 (1): 42 - 51.

104) Ilyasov, R., Gaifullina, L., Saltykova, E., Poskryakov, A and Nikolenko, A. 2012. Review of the expression of antimicrobial peptide defensin in honey bees *Apis Mellifera* L. *Journal of Apicultural Science,* 56: 115.

105) Irish, J., Blair, S and Carter, D. A. 2011. The antibacterial activity of honey derived from Australian flora. *PLoS ONE,* 6: e18229.

106) Isla, M. I., Craig, A., Ordonz, R., Zampini, C., Sayago, J., Bedascarrasbure, E., Alvarez, A., Salomón, V and Maldonado, L. 2011. Physico chemical and bioactive properties of honeys from Northwestern Argentina. *LWT - Food Science and Technology,* 44: 1922 - 1930.

107) Jaganathan, S. K and Mandal, M. 2009. Antiproliferative effects of honey and of its polyphenols: A review. *Journal of Biomedicine and Biotechnology*, 3 (8): 1 - 13.

108) Jageethadevi, A., Saranraj, P. and Ramya, N. 2012. Inhibitory effect of chemical preservatives and organic acids on the growth and organic acids on the growth of bacterial pathogens in poultry chicken. *Asian Journal of Biochemical and Pharmaceutical Research*, 1 (2): 1 - 9

109) Jerkovic, I., Marijanovic, Z and Staver, M. M. 2011. Screening of natural organic volatiles from prunus mahalebl. Honey: Coumarin and vomifoliol as nonspecific biomarkers. *Molecules,* 16: 2507 - 2518.

110) Jerkovic, I., Mastelic, J and Marijanovic, Z. 2006. A variety of volatile compounds as markers in unifloral honey from dalmatian sage (*Salvia officinalis* L.). *Chemistry and Biodiversity,* 3: 1307 - 1316.

111) Jones, R. 2001. Honey and healing through the ages. In Munn P, Jones R (eds): "Honey and Healing". Cardiff: International Bee Research Association, IBRA, pp 1 – 4.

112) Jones, R. 2009. Honey and healing through the ages. *Journal of Api Product and Api Medical Science* 1(1): 2 - 5.

113) Kalidasan, G., Saranraj, P., Ragul, V and Sivasakthi, S. 2017. Antibacterial activity of Natural and Commercial Honey – A comparative study. *Advances in Biological Research*, 11(6): 365 – 372.

114) Kalogeropoulos, N., Konteles, S. J., Troullidou, E., Mourtzinos, I and Karathanos, V. T. 2009. Chemical composition, antioxidant activity and antimicrobial properties of propolis extracts from Greece and Cyprus. *Food Chemistry,* 116, 452 - 461.

115) Kanchana, D., Kavitha, R. and Saranraj, P. 2015. Microbial Spoilage of Modified Atmosphere Packaging on Fruits and Vegetables. *Advances in Biological Research*, 9 (4): 253 – 256.

116) Kanchana, D., Saranraj, P. and Kavitha, R. 2015. Isolation and characterization of some Spoiled Yellow Goat Fish (*Sulphureus cuvier* L.). *World Journal of Fish and Marine Sciences*, 7 (4): 243 – 246.

117) Kandil, A., El - Banby, M., Abdel - Wahed, G. K., Abdel - Gawwad, M., Fayez, M. 1987. Curative properties of true floral and false non-floral honeys on induced gastric ulcers. *Journal of Drug Research*, 17: 103 – 106.

118) Karthikeyan, M., Kanchana, D., Saranraj, P. and Kavi Karunya, S. 2015. Quantification of metabolic products from Lactic acid bacteria isolated from traditional fermented dairy products. *African Education Indices*, 8 (1): 1 – 15.

119) Kaskoniene, V and Venskutonis, P. R. 2010. Floral markers in honey of various botanical and geographic origins: A review. *Comprehensive Reviews in Food Science and Food Safety,* 9: 620 - 634.

120) Katarina, B., Klaudiny, J., Kopernicky, J and Simuth, J. 2002. Identification of honeybee peptide active against *Paenibacillus larvae* larvae through bacterial growth-inhibition assay on polyacrylamide gel. *Apidologie,* 33: 259 - 269.

121) Kingsley, A. 2001. The use of honey in the treatment of infected wound. British Journal of Nursing, 10: S13 - S16.

122) Kirnpal Kaur, B. S., Tan, H. T., Boukraa, L. and Gan, S. H. 2011. Different solid phase extraction fractions of Tualang (*Koompassia excelsa*) honey demonstrated diverse antibacterial properties against wound and enteric bacteria. *Journal of Apiproduct and Apimedical Science*, 3 (1): 59 - 65.

123) Klaudiny, J., Albert, S., Bachanova, K., Kopernicky, J and Simuth, J. 2005. Two structurally different defensin genes, one of them encoding a novel defensin isoform, are expressed in honeybee *Apis mellifera. Insect Biochemistry and Molecular Biology,* 35: 11 - 22.

124) Kolanjinathan, K and Saranraj, P. 2015. Pharmacological activity of Mangrove medicinal plants against pathogenic bacteria and fungi. *Academic Discourse: An International Journal*, 8 (1): 1 – 15.

125) Kolanjinathan, K. and Saranraj, P. 2014. Pharmacological efficacy of marine seaweed *Gracilaria edulis* against clinical pathogens. *Global Journal of Pharmacology*, 8 (2): 268 – 274.

126) Kolanjinathan, K., Ganesh, P., Saranraj, P. and Sekar, D. 2013. Antimicrobial activity of *Gracilaria folifera* extract against pathogenic microorganisms. *International Journal of Current Biochemistry and Biotechnology*, 2 (1): 6 – 9.

127) Kubota, M., Tsuji, M., Nishimoto, M., Wongchawalit, J., Okuyama, M., Mori, H., Matsui, H., Surarit, R., Svasti, J., Kimura, A and Chiba, S. 2004. Localization of α-glucosidases I, II, and III in organs of European honeybees,

Apis mellifera L., and the origin of α-glucosidase in honey. *Bioscience, Biotechnology, and Biochemistry,* 68: 2346 - 2352.

128) Kucuk, M., Kolayli, S., Karaoglu, S., Ulusoy, E., Baltaci, C. and Candan, F. 2007. Biological activities and chemical composition of three honeys of different types from Anatolia. *Food Chemistry*, 100: 526 - 534.

129) Kwakman, P. H. S and Zaat, S. A. J. 2012. Antibacterial components of honey. *IUBMB Life,* 64, 48-55.

130) Kwakman, P. H., Te Velde, A. A., De Boer, L., Speijer, D., Vandenbroucke-Grauls, C. M and Zaat, S. A. 2010. How honey kills bacteria. *FASEB Journal,* 24: 2576 - 2582.

131) Laid Boukraa. 2008. Synergistic action of starch and honey against *Candida albicans* in correlation with diastase number. *Brazilian Journal of Microbiology*, 39: 40 - 43.

132) Levy, S. B and Marshall, B. 2004. Antibacterial resistance worldwide: causes, challenges and responses. *Nature Medicine,* 10: S122 – S129.

133) Lin, L. Z and Harnly, J. M. 2007. A screening method for the identification of glycosylated flavonoids and other phenolic compounds using a standard analytical approach for all plant materials. *Journal of Agricultural and Food Chemistry,* 55: 1084 - 1096.

134) Liu, Ai-Lin, Liu, B., Qin, H. L., Lee, S. M., Wang, Y. T. and Du, G. H. 2008. Anti-influenza virus activities of flavonoids from the medicinal plant *Elsholtzia rugulosa. Planta Medica*, 74 (8): 847 - 851.

135) Lotfy, M., Badra, G., Burham, W and Alenzi, F. Q. 2006. Combined use of honey, bee propolis and myrrh in healing a deep, infected wound in a patient with diabetes mellitus. *Brazilian Journal of Biomedical Science*, 63: 171 - 173.

136) Lusby, P. E., Coombes, A. and Wilkinson, J. M. 2002. Honey: A potent agent for wound healing? *Journal of Wound Ostomy Continence Nursing*, 29: 295 - 300.

137) Mandal, S., Deb Mandal, M. and Pal, N. K. 2010. Synergistic anti-*Staphylococcus aureus* activity of amoxicillin in combination with *Emblica officinalis* and *Nymphae odorata* extracts. *Asian Pacific Journal of Tropical Medicine*, 3: 711 - 714.

138) Mandal, S., Pal, N. K., Chowdhury, I. H. and Deb Mandal, M. 2009. Antibacterial activity of ciprofloxacin and trimethoprim, alone and in combination, against *Vibrio cholerae* O1 biotype El Tor serotype Ogawa isolates. *Polish Journal of Microbiology*, 58: 57 - 60.

139) Manyi Loh, C. E., Clarke, A. M and Ndip, R. N. 2011. An overview of honey: Therapeutic properties and contribution in nutrition and human health. *African Journal of Microbiology Research,* 5(8): 844 - 852.

140) Manyi Loh, C. E., Clarke, A. M and Ndip, R. N. 2012. Detection of phytoconstituents in column fractions of n-hexane extract of gold crest honey exhibiting Anti-*Helicobacter pylori* activity. *Archives of Medical Research,* 43: 197 - 204.

141) Manyi Loh, C. E., Clarke, A. M., Green, E and Ndip, R. N. 2013. Inhibitory and bactericidal activity of selected South African honeys and their solvent extracts against *Helicobacter pylori*. *Pakistan Journal of Pharmaceutical Sciences,* 26: 897 - 906.

142) Manyi Loh, C. E., Ndip, R. N and Clarke, A. M. 2011. Volatile compounds in honey: A review on their involvement in aroma, botanical origin determination and potential biomedical activities. *International Journal of Molecular Sciences,* 12: 9514 - 9532.

143) Mateo, R and Bosch Reig F. 1998. Classification of Spanish Unifloral Honeys by Discriminant Analysis of Electrical Conductivity, Color, Water Content, Sugars, and pH. *Journal of Agriculture and Food Chemistry*, 46: 393 - 400.

144) Mathews, K. A and Binnington A. G. 2002. Wound management using honey. *Journal of Veterinary Science and Technology,* 24: 53 - 60.

145) Mato, I., Huidobro, J. F., Simal Lozano, J and Sancho, M. T. 2003. Significance of non-aromatic organic acids in honey. *Journal of Food Protection,* 66(12): 2371 - 2376.

146) Matsunaga, S., Fusetani, N and Konosu, S. 1985. Bioactive marine metabolites VII. Structures of discodermins B, C, and D, antimicrobial peptides from the marine sponge discodermia kiiensis. *Tetrahedron Letters,* 26: 855 - 856.

147) Mavric, E., Wittmann, S and Henle, T. 2008. Identification and quantification of methyl glyoxal as the dominant antibacterial constituent of manuka (*Leptospermum scoparium*) honeys from New Zealand. *Molecular Nutrition and Food Research*, 52: 483 - 489.

148) Melliou, E and Chinou, I. 2011. Chemical constituents of selected unifloral Greek bee-honeys with antimicrobial activity. *Food Chemistry,* 129: 284 - 290.

149) Miki Fukuda. 2011. Jungle Honey Enhances Immune Function and Antitumor Activity, Hindawi Publishing Corporation, Evidence-Based Complementary and Alternative Medicin, Article ID 908743, 8.

150) Miorin, P. L, Levy Junior, N. C., Custodio, A. R., Bretz, W. A. and Marcucci, M. C. 2003. Antibacterial activity of honey and propolis from *Apis mellifera* and *Tetragonisca angustula* against *Staphylococcus aureus. Journal of Applied Microbiology*, 95: 913 - 920.

151) Misirlioglu, A and Eroglu, S. 2003. Use of honey as an adjunct in the healing of split-thickness skin graft donor sites. *Dermatology Surgery*, 29: 168 - 172.

152) Mohapatra, D. P., Thakur, V and Brar, S. K. 2011. Antibacterial efficacy of raw and processed honey. *Biotechnology Research International,* 20: 1 - 6.

153) Mohd Nasir, Ai-Lin; Liu, B., Qin, H. L., Lee, S. M., Wang, Y. T. and Du, G. H. 2008. Anti-influenza virus activities of flavonoids from the medicinal plant *Elsholtzia rugulosa*. *Planta Medica*, 74 (8): 847 - 851.

154) Molan P. C and Allen, K. L. 1996. The effect of gamma-irradiation on the antibacterial activity of honey. *Journal of Pharmacogeny and Pharmacology,* 48 (11): 1206 - 1209.

155) Molan, P. C. 1992. The antibacterial nature of honey. The nature of the antibacterial activity. *Bee World*, 73: 5 - 28.

156) Molan, P. C. 2001. Why honey is effective as a medicine. 1. Its use in modern medicine. In "Honey and Healing," ed. P. Munn and R. Jones. International Bee Research Association, Cardiff, UK.

157) Molan, P. C. 2006. The evidence supporting the use of honey as a wound dressing. *International Journal of Low Extreme Wounds*, 5: 40 - 54.

158) Molan, P. C. and Cooper, R. A. 2000. Honey and sugar as a dressing for wounds and ulcers. *Tropical Doctor*, 30: 249 - 250.

159) Morais, M., Moreira, L., Feas, X and Estevinho, L. M. 2011. Honey bee - collected pollen from five Portuguese Natural Parks: Palynological origin, phenolic content, antioxidant properties and antimicrobial activity. *Food and Chemical Toxicology,* 49: 1096 - 1101.

160) Mundo, M. A., Padilla – Zakour, O. I and Worobo, R. W. 2004. Growth inhibition of food borne pathogens and food spoilage organisms by select raw honeys. *International Journal of Food Microbiology*, 97: 1 - 8.

161) Murugan, T. and Saranraj, P. 2011. Antibacterial activity of various solvent extracts of the Indian herbal plant *Acalypha indica* against human pathogens causing nosocomial infection. *International Journal of Pharmaceutical and Biological Archives*, 2 (5): 1498 – 1503.

162) Nafisi, S., Hashemi, M., Rajabi, M; Tajmir Riahi, H. A. 2008. DNA adducts with antioxidant flavonoids: morin, apigenin, and naringin. *DNA Cell Biology*, 27 (8): 433 - 442.

163) Nakajima, Y., Ishibashi, J., Yukuhiro, F., Asaoka, A., Taylor, D and Yamakawa, M. 2003. Antibacterial activity and mechanism of action of tick defensin against Gram-positive bacteria. *Biochimica et Biophysica Acta,* 1624: 125 - 130.

164) Natarajan, S., Williamson, D., Grey, J., Harding, K. G. and Cooper, R. A. 2001. Healing of an MRSA-colonized hydroxyurea-induced leg ulcer with honey. *Journal of Dermatology Treatment*, 12: 33 - 36.

165) Newman, D. J and Cragg, G. M. 2007. Natural products as sources of new drugs over the last 25 years. *Journal of Natural Products,* 70: 461 - 477.

166) Newman, D. J and Cragg, G. M. 2012. Natural products as sources of new drugs over the 30 years from 1981 to 2010. *Journal of Natural Products,* 75: 311 - 335.

167) Nicholson, P. T and Shaw, I. 2000. Ancient Egyptian materials and technology. Cambridge University Press; Cambridge, UK.

168) O′Farrelly, C., Branton, D. and Wanke, C. A. 1992. Oral ingestion of egg yolk immunoglobulin from hens immunized with an enterotoxigenic *Escherichia coli* strain prevents diarrhea in rabbits challenged with the same strain. *Infection and Immunity*, 60 (7): 2593 - 2597.

169) O'Neill, J. 2014. Antimicrobial resistance: Tackling a crisis for the health and wealth of nation.

170) Oddo, L. P., Piro, R., Bruneau, E., Guyot Declerck, C., Ivanov, T., Piskulova, J., Flamini, C., Lheritier, J., Morlot, M and Russmann, H. 2004. Main European unifloral honeys: descriptive sheets. *Apidologie,* 35: S38 - S81.

171) Orsolic, N., Knezevic, A. H., Sver, L., Terzic, S., Heckenberger, B. K and Basic, I. 2013. Influence of honey bee products on transplantable murine tumours. *Veterinary and Oncology*, 1: 216 - 226.

172) Osho, A and Bello, O. O. 2010. Antimicrobial effect of honey produced by *Apis mellifera* on some common human pathogens. *Asian Journal of Experimental Biology and Science*, 1(4): 875 - 880.

173) Pawlowska, M. and Armstrong, D. W. 1994. Evaluation of enantiomeric purity of selected amino acids in honey. Chirality, 6: 270 - 276.

174) Peralta, R. C., Yokoyama, H., Ikemori, Y., Kuroki, M. and Kodama, Y. 1994. Passive immunization against experimental salmonellosis in mice by orally administered hen egg-yolk antibodies specific for 14-kDa fimbriae of *Salmonella enteritidis*. *Journal of Medical Microbiology*, 41: 29 – 35.

175) Perez Martin, R. A., Vela Hortiguela, L., Lorenzo Lozano, P., Rojo Cortina, M. D. and De Lorenzo Carretero, C 2008. *In vitro* antioxidant and antimicrobial activities of Spanish honeys. *International Journal of Food Properties*, 11 (4): 727 - 737.

176) Pinho, E., Ferreira, I. C., Barros, L., Carvalho, A. M., Soares, G and Henriques, M. 2014. Antibacterial potential of northeastern Portugal wild plant extracts and respective phenolic compounds. *Biomed Research International,* 81: 45 - 90.

177) Pontes, M., Marques, J. C and Camara, J. S. 2007. Screening of volatile composition from Portuguese multifloral honeys using headspace solid-phase microextraction - gas chromatography-quadrupole mass spectrometry. *Talanta,* 74: 91 - 103.

178) Potts, S. G., Biesmeijer, J. C., Kremen, C., Neumann, P., Schweiger, O and Kunin, W. E. 2010. Global pollinator declines: trends, impacts and drivers. *Trends in Ecology and Evolution,* 25: 345 - 353.

179) Prem Kumar, D., Jayanthi, M and Saranraj, P and Kavi Karunya, S. 2015. Effect of Potassium Sorbate on the inhibition of growth of fungi isolated from spoiled Bakery products. *Life Science Archives*, 1 (4): 217 – 222.

180) Pyrzynska, K and Biesaga, M. 2009. Analysis of phenolic acids and flavonoids in honey. *Trends in Analytical Chemistry,* 28: 893 - 902.

181) Rakhi K., Chute, N. G., Deogade, D and Meghna Kawale. 2010. Antimicrobial activity of Indian honey against clinical isolates. *Asiatic Journal of Biotechnology Resources*, 01: 35 - 38.

182) Ratnieks, F. L. W and Carreck, N. L. 2010. Clarity on Honey Bee Collapse? *Science,* 327: 152 - 153.

183) Raupach, B., Mecsas, J., Heczko, U., Falkow, S. and Finlay, B. B. 1999. Bacterial epithelial cell cross talk. *Current Topics in Microbiology and Immunology*, 236: 137 -161.

184) Rosenblat, G., Angonnet, S., Goroshit, A. Tabak, M. and Neeman, I. 1997. Antioxidant properties of honey produced by bees fed with medical plant extracts. In "Proceedings of the International Conference on Bee Products: Properties, Applications and Apitherapy" held in Tel Aviv, Israel, May 26 - 30, p. 49 -55. Plenum Press, New York.

185) Rufian Henares, J. A. and De La Cueva, S. P. 2009. Antimicrobial activity of coffee melanoidins - A study on their metal-chelating properties. *Journal of Agricultural and Food Chemistry*, 57: 432 – 438.

186) Sahl, H. G., Pag, U., Bonness, S., Wagner, S., Antcheva, N and Tossi, A. 2005. Mammalian defensins: structures and mechanism of antibiotic activity. *Journal of Leukocyte Biology*, 77: 466 – 475.

187) Sampath Kumar, K. P., Debjit Bhowmik, Chiranjib, Biswajit and M. R. Chandira. 2010. Medicinal uses and health benefits of Honey: An Overview. *Journal of Chemistry and Pharmacy Research*, 2 (1): 385 – 395.

188) Sanchez, V., Baeza, R., Ciappini, C., Zamora M. C and Chirife, J. 2010. Comparison between Karl Fischer and refractometric method for determination of moisture in honey. *Food Control*, 21: 339 - 341.

189) Saranraj, P. and Ramya, M. 2016. Role of Organic acids and Hydrogen peroxide in fruit juice preservation: A Review. *Journal of Pharmaceutical and Biological Sciences*, 4 (2): 58 – 73.

190) Saranraj, P. and Sivasakthi, S. 2014. Medicinal plants and its antimicrobial properties: A Review. *Global Journal of Pharmacology*, 8(3): 316 - 337

191) Saranraj, P. and Sivasakthivelan, P. 2012. Screening of antibacterial activity of medicinal plant *Phyllanthus amarus* against Urinary tract infection (UTI) causing bacterial pathogens. *Applied Journal of Hygiene*, 1 (3): 19 – 24.

192) Saranraj, P. and Stella, D. 2011. Antibiogram of nosocomial infection and its antimicrobial drug resistance. *International Journal of Pharmaceutical and Biological Archives*, 2 (6): 1598 - 1610.

193) Saranraj, P. and Sujitha, D. 2015. Mangrove Medicinal Plants: A Review. *American – Eurasian Journal of Toxicological Sciences*, 7 (3): 146 – 156.

194) Saranraj, P., Naidu, M. A. and Sivasakthivelan, P. 2013. Lactic acid bacteria and its antimicrobial properties: A Review. *International Journal of Pharmaceutical and Biological Archives*, 4 (6): 1124 - 1133

195) Saranraj, P., Sivasakthi, S and Glaucio Dire Feliciano. 2016. Pharmacology of Honey – A Review. *Advances in Biological Research*, 10 (4): 271 - 289.

196) Saranraj, P., Stella, D and Reetha, D. 2012. Bioactivity of *Mangifera indica* ethanol extract against human pathogenic microorganisms. *Novus International Journal of Pharmaceutical Technology*, 1 (1): 11 - 18.

197) Saranraj, P., Stella, D. and Reetha, D. 2012. Microbial spoilage of vegetables and its control measures: A Review. *International Journal of Natural Product Science*, 2 (2): 1 -12.

198) Saranraj, P., Stella, D., Sathiyaseelan, K. and Sajani Samuel. 2010. Antibacterial potentiality of Ethanol and Ethyl acetate extract of *Acalypha indica* against human pathogenic bacteria. *Journal of Ecobiotechnology*, 2 (7): 23 – 27.

199) Sato, T and Miyata, G. 2000. The Nutraceutical Benefit, Part III: Honey. *Nutrition,* 16: 468 - 469.

200) Schmitt, E. K., Moore, C. M., Krastel, P and Petersen, F. 2011. Natural products as catalysts for innovation: a pharmaceutical industry perspective. *Current Opinion in Chemical Biology,* 15: 497 - 504.

201) Schramm, D. D., Karim, M., Schrader, H. R., Holt, R. R., Cardetti, M. and Keen, C. L. 2003. Honey with high levels of antioxidants can provide protection to healthy human subjects. *Journal of Agricultural and Food Chemistry*, 51: 1732 - 1735.

202) Sekar, D., Kolanjinathan, K., Saranraj, P. and Gajendiran, K. 2012. Screening of *Phyllanthus amarus*, *Acalypha indica* and *Datura metel* for its antimicrobial activity against selected pathogens. *International Journal of Pharmaceutical and Biological Archives*, 3 (5): 1231 - 1236.

203) Sherlock, O., Dolan, A., Athman, R., Power, A., Gethin, G. and Cowman, S. 2010. Comparison of the antimicrobial activity of ulmo honey from Chile and manuka honey against methicillin-resistant *Staphylococcus aureus, Escherichia coli* and *Pseudomonas aeruginosa*. *BMC Complement Alternative Medicine*, 10: 47.

204) Silici, S., Sagdic, O and Ekici, L. 2010. Total phenolic content, antiradical, antioxidant and antimicrobial activities of *Rhododendron* honeys. *Food Chemistry,* 121: 238 - 243.

205) Simon, A., Santos, K., Blaser, G., Bode, U and Molan, P. 2009. Medical honey for wound carestill the 'last resort'? *eCAM*, 6: 165 – 173.

206) Simon, A., Traynor, K., Santos, K., Blaser, G., Bode, U. and Molan, P. 2008. Medical honey for wound care-still the 'Latest Resort'. Evid Based Complement Alternative Medicine, doi:10.1093/ecam/ nem175.

207) Singh, S. B and Barrett, J. F. 2006. Empirical antibacterial drug discovery - Foundation in natural products. *Biochemical Pharmacology,* 71: 1006 - 1015.

208) Siva Sakthi, S., Geetha, M. and Saranraj, P. 2011. Pharmacological screening of *Datura metel* and *Acalypha indica* for its Antifungal activity against fungal pathogens. *International Journal of Pharmaceutical Science and Health Care*, 1 (2): 15 – 30.

209) Siva Sakthi, S., Saranraj, P. and Geetha, M. 2011. Antibacterial evaluation and phytochemical screening of *Datura metel* leaf extracts against bacterial pathogens. *International Journal of Pharmaceutical and Biological Archives*, 2 (4): 1130 - 1136

210) Skiadas, P. K and Lascaratos, J. G. 2001. Dietetics in ancient Greek philosophy: Plato's concepts of healthy diet. *European Journal of Clinical Nutrition*, 55: 532 - 537.

211) Snowden, J. A. and Cliver, D.O. 1996. Microorganisms in honey. *International Journal of Food Microbiology*, 31: 1 - 26.

212) Srisayam, M. and Chantawannakul, P. 2010. Antimicrobial and antioxidant properties of honeys produced by Apis Mellifera in Thailand. *Journal of Apiproduct and Apimedical Science*, 2 (2): 77 - 83.

213) Stinson, E. E., Subers, M. N., Petty, J. and White, J. W. 1963. Separation and identification of the organic acids. *Archives of Biochemistry and Biophysics*, 6: 12.

214) Style, S. 1992. Honey: From Hive to Honeypot. London: Pavilion

215) Subrahmanyam, M. 1991. Topical application of honey in treatment of burns. *Brazilian Journal of Surgery*, 78: 497 – 498.

216) Sumner, L. W., Lei, Z., Nikolau, B. J and Saito, K. 2015. Modern plant metabolomics: advanced natural product gene discoveries, improved technologies, and future prospects. *Natural Product Reports,* 32: 212 - 229.

217) Swellam, T., Miyanaga, N., Onozawa, M., Hattori, K., Kawai, K., Shimazui, T and Akaza, H. 2013. Antineoplastic activity of honey in an experimental bladder cancer implantation model: *in vivo* and *in vitro* studies. *International Journal of Urology*, 10: 213 - 219.

218) Tan, S T., Wilkins, A. L., Holland, P. T. and Mcghie, T. K. 1989. Extractives from New Zealand Unifloral Honeys. 2. Degraded Carotenoids and Other Substances from Heather Honey. *Journal of Agricultural and Food Chemistry*, 37: 1217 - 1221.

219) Tannahill, R. 1975. Food in History. St Albans: Paladin.

220) Taormina, P.J., Niemira, B.A. and Beuchat, L.R. 2001. Inhibitory activity of honey against foodborne pathogens as influenced by the presence of hydrogen peroxide and level of antioxidant power. *International Journal of Food Microbiology*, 69: 217 - 225.

221) Temaru, E., Shimura, S., Amano, K. and Karasawa, T. 2007. Antibacterial activity of honey from stingless honeybees (Hymenoptera; Apidae; Meliponinae). *Polish Journal of Microbiology*, 56 (4): 281 - 285.

222) Terrab. A., Hernanz, D and Heredia, F. J. 2004. Inductively coupled plasma optical emission spectrometric determination of minerals in thyme honeys and their contribution to geographical discrimination. *Journal of Agriculture and Food Chemistry,* 52: 3441- 3445.

223) Tonks, A. J., Cooper, R. A., Jones, K. P., Blair, S., Parton, J. and Tonks, A. 2003. Honey stimulates inflammatory cytokine production from monocytes. *Cytokine*, 21: 242 - 247.

224) Usharani, G., Srinivasan, G., Sivasakthi, S. and Saranraj, P. 2015. Antimicrobial activity of *Spirulina platensis* solvent extracts against pathogenic bacteria and bacteria. *Advances in Biological Research*, 9 (5): 292 – 298.

225) Van den Berg, A. J., Van den Worm, E., Van Ufford, H. C., Halkes, S. B., Hoekstra, M. J. and Beukelman, C. J. 2008. An *in vitro* examination of the antioxidant and anti-inflammatory properties of buckwheat honey. *Journal of Wound Care*, 17: 172 - 178.

226) Van Herpen, T. W. J. M., Cankar, K., Nogueira, M., Bosch, D., Bouwmeester, H. J and Beekwilder, J. 2010. *Nicotiana benthamiana* as a production platform for artemisinin precursors. *PLoS ONE,* 5: e14222.

227) Visavadia, B., Honeysett, J. D and Martin, H. 2009. Manuka honey dressing: An effective treatment for chronic wound infections. *European Journal of Clinical Microbiology and Infectious Disease*, 28: 339 - 344.

228) Viuda Martos, M., Ruiz Navajas, Y., Fernandez Lopez, J. and Perez Alvarez, J. A. 2008. Functional properties of honey, propolis and royal jelly. *Journal of Concise Reviews and Hypotheses in Food Science*, 73 (9): 117 - 124.

229) Vorlova, L., Karpiskova, R., Chabiniokova, I., Kalabova, K. and Brazdova, Z. 2005. The antimicrobial activity of honeys produced in the Czech Republic. *Czech Journal of Animal Science*, 50 (8): 376 - 384.

230) Weston, R. J. 2000. The contribution of catalase and other natural products to the antibacterial activity of honey: A review. *Food Chemistry*, 71: 235 - 239.

231) White, J. W and Subers, M. H. 2013. Studies on honey inhibine, a chemical assay. *Journal of Apiculture Research*, 15: 23 - 28.

232) White, J. W. 1975. Physical characteristics of honey. In: Crane E (ed) Honey, A Comprehensive Survey, Hienemann, London, UK, 207 - 239.

233) White, J. W. 1978. Honey. *Advanced Food Research*, 24: 288 - 374.

234) White, J. W., Subers, M. H. and Schepartz, A. I. 1963. The identification of inhibine. *American Bee Journal*, 102 (11): 430 - 431.

235) WHO. 2014. Antimicrobial resistance: global report on surveillance World Health Organization.

236) Wilkinson, J. M. and Cavanagh, H. M. 2005. Antibacterial activity of 13 honeys against *Escherichia coli* and *Pseudomonas aeruginosa. Journal of Medicine and Food,* 8: 100 -103.

237) Willix, D. J., Molan, P. C. and Harfoot, C. G. 1992. A comparison of the sensitivity of wound - infecting species to the antibacterial activity of manuka honey and other honey. *Journal of Applied Bacteriology*, 73: 388 - 394.

238) Wilson, C. A. 1973. Food and Drink in Britain: From the Stone Age to Recent Times. London: Constable.

239) Wilson, M. B., Spivak, M., Hegeman, A. D., Rendahl, A and Cohen, J. D. 2013. Metabolomics reveals the origins of antimicrobial plant resins collected by honey bees. *PLoS ONE,* 8: e77512.

240) Won, S. R., Li, C. Y., Kim, J. W and Rhee, H. I. 2009. Immunological characterization of honey major protein and its application. *Food Chemistry,* 113: 1334 - 1338.

241) Wooley J. C., Godzik, A and Fredberg, I. 2010. A Primer on Metagenomics. *PLoS Computational Biology,* 6: e1000667.

242) Zappalà, M., Fallico, B., Arena, E and Verzera, A. 2005. Methods for the determination of HMF in honey: A comparison. *Food Control,* 16: 273 - 277.

243) Zeina, B., Othman, O. and Al-Assad, S. 1996. Effect of honey versus thyme on Rubella virus survival *in vitro. Journal of Alternative and Complementary Medicine,* 2 (3): 345 - 348.

244) Zumla A. and Lulat A. 1989. Honey - a remedy rediscovered. *Journal of Social Medicine,* 82: 384 - 385.

www.ingramcontent.com/pod-product-compliance
Lightning Source LLC
Chambersburg PA
CBHW080217170726
48282CB00030B/1149
9789391342210